THE WORLD IS NOT ENDING B̶U̶T̶

THE ONLY BC
R

INTROL

This book has been written as a factual reference to the true origin and ancient history of mankind, unlike the story we have been lead to believe. A comprehensive picture of exactly what is happening today in our troubled world and the precarious future that awaits us and how we can prepare. Whilst reading the book you must disengage from all stereotypical ways you have been programmed to think and look at the book as a factual time line of history, renewing human history, piecing together this world's predicament and how our situation is escalating into a non-reversible state of decline and controlled human freedom. The aim of this book is to guide your thoughts and open your eyes to a different perspective giving you the chance to reach your own conclusion on the ruling class and the true agenda that awaits us all.

AUTHOR JACK GREY

PUBLISHED 23 FEBRUARY 2018

CONTENTS

Chapter 1 7
- The True Origin of Mankind 10
- The Sumerian Story 17
- The Father of Occultism and Worship of Baphomet.....33
- The Timeline of Humanity 39

Chapter 2 67
- The Six Heads of the Dragon 67

Chapter 3 93
- Understanding England's Perspective 93

Chapter 4 102
- The Blueprint Connection 102

Chapter 5 127
- The Implications of Disaster 127

Chapter 6 137
- Our Future 137
- What is the Human Race? 146
- What the Near Future Holds and the Direct Implications For You 152

Chapter 7 159
- The Secrets of Alchemy and Hermetic Philosophy......159

Conclusion 166

THE WORLD IS NOT ENDING BUT ...

The world is ending but 5 billion years from now, not last Friday or a week Tuesday as some have predicted. The Sun will eventually deplete of fuel, burning itself out and finally becoming a White Dwarf star and when this happens we will have a problem. As the human race accelerates to a large and crucial juncture in its existence, we need to take stock of our situation and examine exactly what is happening behind closed doors in our troubled times, of which the vast majority of the world's population is mostly oblivious and also how it will affect you, the people, directly. Since the beginning of civilisation, the control of the ruling class has shaped our lives and it's more prevalent now than it ever was. With egotistical leaders and world order groups, the true governors of our times, it seems apparent their aims remain the same and have not changed for the last 7,000 years. Namely strict social and economic control of the masses, the endless search for immortality, the Holy Grail and the seeking of the lost knowledge. It is unlikely the facts of our true origin or our precarious future will ever be revealed in the public domain but kept in the inner circle.

We are only just scratching the surface of understanding the knowledge that has been left to us in the forms of hieroglyphic symbolism, sacred sciences and the esoteric techniques of ancient worlds. Before the Great Flood our forefathers had the knowledge and understanding of the concepts of other dimensions and the gateway to the afterlife.

Using key points of archaeological factual evidence, I would like to take you on a journey revealing the true origin of our species. Not that of the fabled creator who lives on a cloud, but secrets of our consciousness, our being and the true meaning and purpose of our existence. As I am hesitant to believe anything unless fact or proven, disregard any stereotypical concepts and beliefs ingrained within, by media influence and tradition which you hold whilst reading this book and treat it as historic fact. Although many sources have conflicting time periods, a picture has emerged which certainly casts doubt and distrust of the ruling class. The beliefs and laws by which we have lived our lives for centuries is a means of control and extortion of the masses which is often at the heart of most war and disorder throughout time.

One of the most important events we need to be aware of today is the potential threat involving the passing of our 10th planet Eris, also known in the Sumerian tablets as Nibiru. The 10th planet which has only just been publicly acknowledged in 2016, although known to the few for hundreds of years, has an orbit around our sun which occurs every 3,600 years and is approaching close to earth in the very near future.

One of the biggest questions that seems to be unanswered is whether we are the first or the last planet with an atmosphere. We have numerous satellites travelling in outer space searching for new planets where we could perhaps live in the future when our planet comes to its end. But to date we have found only one which is so distant it is impossible to even consider or comprehend the possibility of travelling there, let alone the dream of habitation.

We are definitely not the first civilisation to have inhabited Earth, evidenced by the vast amounts of archaeological structures and relics which have been found dating back thousands of years. Earth is the last planet in our galaxy and neighbouring space which has surface habitation, so in fact we are the last. All planets except the gas giants are made of a similar structure and would have gone through a similar evolution to Earth as they formed at the same time according to scientific belief. But something happened to their atmosphere perhaps very similar to what is happening today on Earth with the ozone being destroyed by pollution. The decay of the ozone layer does not happen overnight, it is a gradual process which in the end will render the surface of our planet uninhabitable for human existence. When this process occurs the only option, unless our civilisation is advanced enough to rocket off into another dimension or travel at the speed of light in a huge vessel, will be to live underground.

Our Moon does not spin, it stays facing the same direction and rotates round the Earth with the 'dark side of the moon' facing away, meaning we are unable to view that side. Photos emerged in the 1960s producing images of the reverse side showing old flowing river beds and rock formations suggesting it was, at some point, able to sustain life with water and bacteria in abundance, the same evolution as on Earth. It is certain that some kind of living organisms having light and water are living beneath the surface and within the outer core of other planets. It remains to be seen how advanced these life forms are and if intelligent life in fact lives inside our neighbouring rocks following the demise of their atmosphere.

CHAPTER 1

In 1849 in Iraq a British archaeologist named Austin Henry Layard discovered the most important historic find which changed our perception of ancient history forever and brought doubt on the knowledge we had been taught. Twenty-two thousand clay tablets along with a cache of pottery, mosaics and jewellery were unearthed. It was not until the 1970s that a man called Zachariah Sitchin spent his life deciphering the artefacts which were found.

The writing was in a form called Cuneiform, a system using wooden shaped objects pushed into clay then baked in fire to make them durable. This race of people is known as the Sumerians, they built some of the first commercial cities after the great flood around 9,600 BC, with evidence proving their existence dating back to 7,000 BC.

Amongst the clay tablets there were drawings showing the creation of man. They describe how a race of people visited Earth from another dimension or planet. The Sumerians named these people 'The Anunnaki' which translated means 'Those who came from the sky'. The hieroglyphs show a superior race of giant beings in control of earth and depicting the planetary geography of our galaxy plus one more planet called Nibiru, making ten, which is one more than originally thought until recently. The picture gives incredible detail of the proportional dimensions and order in which the planets align. In the mainstream teaching of history, the people of this time had simple lives living in mud huts and gathering berries with simple wheat crops, not using intergalactic telescopes or having knowledge of our galaxy. So how was this knowledge gained?

When the Sumerian and Egyptian cultures are studied, according to the history that is taught to us, it is apparent that these dominating cultures seemed to start with great knowledge and architecture and slowly declined not the other way around.

All that we have been taught concerning our early origin is a complete fabrication. The Bible, a best seller, is a plagiarised version of ancient stories produced by the Roman hierarchy in 325 AD as a guide to the people, as a moral code to live by and a rule book to suppress and control the direction of the masses. You cannot totally dismiss all of the scriptures written in the bible as many have been directly copied from previous ancient scriptures but they should not be taken literally word for word. Fortunately for us there were many scribes in the past who were recording history on stone tablets and papyrus who were recognised as reliable historic sources distinct from the religious writings.

I have focused on the great thinkers and scribes of ancient times such as Enoch, Socrates, Pythagoras, Plato and Aristotle, who wrote contemporary history and stories of their forgotten past. One thing they all have in common is their practise of alchemy, the search for the 'Philosophers Stone' which is not just making gold from base metal as many people believe. In the dark ages, alchemists were known for trying to transform lead into gold. You must be aware that they were the great thinkers and scientists of their time discovering things that were considered the work of the devil or heresy punishable by death or imprisonment. When the Catholic Church declared war on people that studied science, philosophy and spiritualism, the great alchemists adopted a code to protect themselves from the persecution of the church and the later inquisition.

The search was for the elixir of life that would bring rejuvenation and immortality for mankind. Alchemists believed that the process of purification of any elements would lead to perfection. Not only making gold from lead, for example but also searching for the purification of our soul and conscious being, so as to gain higher understanding and spiritual fulfilment leading to the afterlife. The process of purification of metal elements originally evolved from the ancient Hermetic traditions and teachings.

A book of alchemy, Mutus Liber, edited in 1676 was published, consisting of illustrations regarding alchemical methods. To the uninitiated this book appears to be a bizarre pictorial story of fictional characters, but those who were familiar with alchemy would be able to understand the meaning behind the illustrations as no words where used. The whole process of transmutation through purification can be observed in this book showing that the laws of nature and its basic creative elements have all the answers to the 'the twelve stages of transmutation'. Many ancient texts are plagued with pictorial and symbolic notes to keep the knowledge alive a little longer and passing it on to the next generation. This is why so much information is misunderstood and badly translated. In those days only 5% of people were literate, because to be able to study was a privilege that came at a cost and so the knowledge of the forefathers was often handed down by word of mouth, with some becoming distorted.

THE TRUE ORIGIN OF MANKIND

The Sumerians were the first recorded educated race of people found to date well before the Aztecs, Mayan or Greek civilisations situated in the Middle East now named Iraq. This is where the story begins although I must backtrack to make the facts more understandable. The false belief and doctrine of contemporary religion started at the death of Jesus Christ although his true Hebrew name was Yeshua given to him at birth, the name Jesus was taken from the Greek translation.

After the Romans and the Jewish Zionists, the corrupt money people of the time in Jerusalem, decided Jesus was a threat to their power and thriving trade so they crucified him. He was thought to have died but he rose from the dead and his followers spread the word that if you follow his teachings, you will in return have everlasting life with his father in Heaven.

The Romans, at this stage the leading power, still believed and worshipped many different gods. Monotheism was against their belief but in 312 AD on 28 October Constantine the Emperor of Rome published the first Bible changing their religion to the Christian belief and started the Roman Catholic Church as it still is today. Rome in those days was ruled from Constantinople, today's Istanbul. The Bible was compiled by Constantine using various scripts from ancient sources producing a believable story which suited his purpose of rule over the people, so the religion began. The book was changed over the centuries and the first English written Bible that people adhere to today was the King James translation in 1611 AD in which the stories are still used to day as their gospel.

The most important fact which was omitted was the use of the original historic texts found in the 'Book of Enoch' and the Jewish Torah, the first true written scripts. The whole concept of our true beginning, which will be explained shortly, was never used as it was thought to be too controversial to start a believable religion. In 1946 sections of the old Hebrew bible were found in Wadi Qumran near the Dead Sea in an old pottery vessel hidden in a cave, near Jerusalem, now named 'The Dead Sea Scrolls'. These scrolls were the true words of this time in history and describe a story which has been clearly altered by contemporary bible writers. The news of Jesus having a wife and a brother and perhaps children has challenged the Christian belief but puts the whole concept of religion into perspective.

In the early days religion or worship began more peacefully with people being aware of the seasons and their crop cycles, showing respect to the sun and stars with festivals and rituals like the harvest festival we still have today. They were living in rhythm with nature believing that the only real god was the one they could feel and see, the sun, the giver of life to all things, and the pagan religion began. As man's imagination grew we invented new gods for different seasons and different beliefs so around the world many different cultures formed their own rituals and beliefs. Then something happened.

After researching cultures from around the world a pattern formed with various worldwide events showing up in all cultures at the same time as far back as 11,000 years ago. The most famous of course was the deluge, the Big Flood in the Noah story. Noah and his boat may well be a myth as no evidence has ever been discovered but the event itself, a worldwide catastrophe most certainly shows up around 9,600 BC evidentially in the layers of silt in the earth. Near the Dead Sea next to the believed Sodom and Gomorrah ruins is a sheer cliff showing our past in layers of silt, one of the best examples in the world showing the climate patterns of our past. It shows at this time a huge change in our atmospheric conditions. What actually happened then we will probably never know for sure but what we are certain of is that it had a huge impact on the human population wiping clean the surface of the Earth and covering it with sea.

Before the Great Flood the geography of the planet was very different, whether it was a meteor hitting Earth or some huge natural event caused by volcanic activity the result was the same, the world was destroyed. Water levels rose and covered everything in its wake. As technology develops in underwater exploration we are finding dozens of lost cities all round the world which have been lost for centuries. Off the west coast of India in the Gulf of Cambay, submerged in the sea, two huge cities were found in 2001 thought to be Myth, home to the Indian god Krishna. These discoveries have been dated to at least 12000 years ago, before the flood, throwing mainstream archaeology into dispute. Off the coast of Egypt the legendary city of Alexandria was found beneath the ocean, the most important keystone to understanding ancient mediterranean history, the great ship port and library, still being excavated today. The answer to the future is in the past, the future is not here yet. Many historians underestimate man's abilities and the great architecture they achieved in the past.

At this point in history we lost a great civilisation, a great race of people highly advanced but in a different direction to ourselves, focused on nature, astrology, vibration technology, the afterlife, connecting with nature and the earth's energy.

So where did the technology to create such sophisticated buildings like the Great Pyramid of Giza and many other such structures around the world come from? Although our historic teachings seem to focus on Egypt as being the main ancient civilisation where the great architects and keepers of the lost knowledge lived, there are hundreds of pyramids all round the world. Positioned in most continents they form a geometric grid, although the purpose is thought to be an ancient power system or vibration technology, the truth is still unknown. In many ways we are just catching up with what our forefathers already new. My belief, based on factual study along with other historians, is that the knowledge of the old world was carried on by the survivors of the deluge and was used to start over again building new towns and cities after the world's chaos had settled. The secret knowledge of our past world and esoteric teachings were kept at this point by the new rulers and the chosen blood lines of the Anunnaki.

Our religious books tell us that man first started in the Garden of Eden 4,004 BC although contradictory to Darwin's 'Theory of Evolution' where Darwin suggests we evolved from monkeys/primates dating back to 65,000 years ago. Evolution is present throughout the natural world and species move forward through environmental change. But the so-called missing link has never been found, the reason being there is not one. Not wanting to get too deep into the biological make up of our DNA and chromosomes, the idea of ape becoming man is biologically impossible.

Whilst studying history we must consider that one family unit, from grandfather to grandson, stretches 150 years. It is only two 'families' ago in England that the Catholic Church was burning women at the stake for being witches and only 13 families ago that Christ was born. The origin of man is estimated to be 165 million years old but we are struggling to find solid evidence of past history beyond 12,000 years ago.

Zachariah Sitchin a respected man in his field of archaeology, has spent the last 50 years studying and deciphering the Sumerian tablets searching for the answer of man's true genesis and confirms my beliefs and studies that a superior race of people was present on earth before the Great Flood.

After the deluge, it is believed that a place called Eden, pronounced ee/dan in the past, in southern Iraq which lies between the Euphrates River and the Tigress River is the place that mankind regrouped and started to live again after the Flood. Sumur a proven city in Sumeria was located in Iraq 6,000 years ago. On one of the clay tablets it describes this civilisation in great detail referring to it as a thriving trade city with vast infrastructure, written law, art and literature, a cultured civilisation developed in a relatively short period of time. These people already had vast knowledge pre-dating the basic idea of Adam and Eve starting the world. Throughout this period of 4,000 years, man still had not learnt the concept of love and peace and through the eradication of fine libraries through war, the written texts of our forefathers, which held the knowledge of the past, was lost through time.

It was the Sumerians who first used or continued to use the mathematical structure of time turning 60 seconds to a minute, 60 minutes in an hour, 360 degrees in a circle and so on. They also developed their own writing system called Cuneiform. Many historic events like ledgers from tradesmen, contracts from business people and general documentation were also among the tablets found. They wrote on the tablets that this knowledge was given to them by 'the people who came from the sky', The Anunnaki.

The symbol of 'Vesica Piscis' which is used today symbolising the first atoms that were formed in the making of the universe was drawn by these people. These same symbols are found throughout the world, the most famous being the stone Chinese lions which guard exotic gateways, the carved ball under the right foot is the pattern of the 'flower of life' and these date back to the Flood. Although the Arab States have unearthed some amazing pieces of ancient architecture which has changed man's understanding of our distant past, the Chinese, the worshippers of the dragon, still hold many treasures which are deemed religious sites and are prohibited from excavation by the authorities.

An astrological event that happened on 8 March 2012 puts all that we know into perspective and doubt in the understanding and theories of our universe. Televised throughout the world images and video footage were shown on live TV of an unknown object docking on the edge of the sun. The surface of the sun is 27 million degrees Fahrenheit. The unknown entity which can only be described as resembling a hard-skinned jelly fish was captured by NASA's satellite cameras which circumnavigate the sun. The object slowly moved towards the sun's corona with its long protruding tail attaching itself to the sun. It has been calculated to be the size of the Earth. It stayed there for 80 hours looking as if it was drawing energy from the radiation plumes of the sun, then eventually pushed of like a leaping frog breaking the connection and firing off into space at a rapid rate.

We have heard nothing since this event of any explanation of what it may be or in fact if it may be heading this way. What are we not being told? If you missed the very short transmission on public media of this event, please take time to view and come to your own conclusion. (Ref.Sec.4)

THE SUMERIAN STORY

The general story laid out by the Sumerian tablets tells of history dating back some 430,000 years. It tells of a superior race of people who visited Earth and lived on planet Nibiru, the same planet which is due to pass earth on its orbit of the sun which happens every 3,600 years. The writings suggest that the Anunnaki came to earth to mine for gold which was needed to help the dwindling atmosphere on their planet. The Anunnaki brought civilisation to earth twice, once before the Flood and again afterwards to restart civilisation. These beings were of large stature seen as giants to earthlings and were divine, living for thousands of years. This visitation and world control is the true genesis of our past where religion and the thought of eternal life began. If you cut through the fog of religious doctrine and consider the legacy of the divine Anunnaki many things become clear. They left our planet around 4,100 BC leaving their bloodline to control Earth and collect gold. They stated they will return in the passing of Pisces and the beginning of the Age of Aquarius when their planet passes us again in orbit, between Jupiter and Mars. The holders of the gold are promised eternal life, the holders of our gold rule our world.

We are a very delicate species and extremely vulnerable to any sophisticated outside intelligent intervention. Our whole world is held together by the world web and computer communication, one sonic wave of extreme electrical power would render the world's population defenceless. If the Anunnaki are returning, if another race was here before, as written in 'The King Ship' and many other documents, I feel it will not be beneficial for us as a race, in fact the opposite. As a realist I feel that they would be returning to reap their seeds as they did before, not to give everyone a big kiss.

The Anunnaki Gods in the scriptures seem to be an arrogant, aggressive race of people having constant wars on Nibiru and Mars, as well as Earth. The pyramid structures were seen as a great prize for whoever ruled them and this caused a series of wars known as the 'Pyramid Wars' in the Sumerian Tablets. 'The Sumerian Cylinder Seal' depicts the victory of the Anunnaki Utu, winning the battle for the pyramids, suggesting that the original pyramids of Giza were built much earlier.

After their failure to extract gold from the waters of the Persian Gulf they set up base in seven different areas of the world and more Anunnaki came to help with the quest, with 600 strong they started to mine gold in South Africa. It tells of a mutiny amongst their people involving the hardship of collecting gold. Anu the leader at this time suggests they should not abandon their efforts to mine gold but instead genetically change the creatures on earth, enough to make them strong but able to be controlled.

The 'Creation Cylinder Seal' describes the trial and errors of Anu trying to combine Anunnaki and the earthly primate genes to create a hybrid and according to the texts they succeeded in creating what we are today. This sounds very similar to 'And he took the rib from Adam and made woman' from the biblical texts. The writings describing 'The Seven Tablets of Creation' are parallel to the biblical account of Genesis, although written some

4,000 years before. They made us in their own image, these people taught us the knowledge of galaxies, architecture and the ways of agriculture, they gave man civilisation.

Out of the many incredible artefacts that where recovered from sites in Iraq where flourishing Sumerian cities once stood, was the intriguing Sumerian King List, an ancient manuscript originally recorded in the Sumerian language. It lists the Kings of Sumer from Sumeria and neighbouring dynasties giving their reign lengths and the locations of their empires or kingship. What makes this artefact so unique is the fact that the list blends with other sources of dynastic rulers in historic records which are known to have existed. Egyptian kings, we are told, date back to only 3,100 BC with the first King being Pharaoh Menes but this is untrue.

'The King Ship' scribes were found by Herbert Weld-Blundell in Larsa, home of the fourth antediluvian King Kichunna, a few miles north of Ur, a major historic city in Mesopotamia. A clay prism 8 inches high with four sides and two columns on each side. It was written in Cuneiform around 2,170 BC by a scribe who signed as Nur-Ninsubur from the end of the Isin dynasty (displayed today in the Cuneiform Dynasty collection, Ashmolean Museum, Oxford, UK). It is one of the most extensive and complete lists of our past ancient kings and nobles. It is believed to have had a central spindle originally made of wood so that the stone list could be turned and viewed easily. The

Sumerian King List begins with the very origin of a divine leadership which had descended from the sky, as their dynasties lasted for thousands of years unlike man.

Sumeria was the site of at least twelve separate cities namely Nippur, Adab, Umma, Kish, Erech, Ur, Sippar, Akshak, Larak, Lagash, Bad-tibira, and Larsa. After the Flood these cities become the rebirth of civilisation and, although the people at first were free to live, control was quickly taken by the Anunnaki kings. The Sumerian King List records that eight kings with a total of 241,200 years ruled from the time when the Anunnaki descended to earth until the Great Flood, namely Eridug, Alulim, Alaljar Annu as well as others.

A green emerald tablet was discovered separately, although still in Iraq, revealing spiritual technology encoded within the tablet's mysterious writings. The formula shows very specific esoteric teachings showing how to achieve personal transformation and even accelerate the evolution of our species. This artefact was translated into Greek in Alexandria's time displayed in Egypt around 330 BC although this is the last time it was seen. Copies of the stone fortunately, can be seen in most reputable museums round the world with English translation. The emerald tablet contains secret formulas, which many of the alchemists used to meditate and achieve higher states of altered consciousness.

According to Eusebius of Caesarea, who was a Roman historian of Greek descent, a dynasty of gods ruled Egypt for 13,900 years: the first was the god Vulcan, after Sosis of the Sun, Isis and Osiris of Saturn, Typhoon brother of Osiris, and Horus the son of Isis and Osiris. They were followed by a dynasty of demigods, the bloodline of the Anunnaki who ruled for 11,025 years. Hereafter in 3,100 BC, the first human pharaoh would rule over Egypt. The headdresses and ritual clothing found in the 'Valley of the Kings' the burial place of the later pharaohs, were items used to mimic the ancient gods in rituals hoping for eternal life themselves.

Geneticists who study the geographic side of DNA from different cultures throughout time have claimed that our genetic creation and origin comes from South Africa, the same place as the Anunnaki first started to mine gold. Many structures and strange anomalies are being excavated today in the southern gold regions of Africa concentrating on orbital ruins and underground shafts which have been found revealing an ancient commercial civilisation.

The Book of Enoch and much other historic literature from all corners of the earth holds the same story of the Nephilim, the supposed fallen angels talked about in the bible. The Nephilim was the Anunnaki who mated with the genetically modified human and produced a species of giants. The Nephilim were believed to be divine although their offspring were only demigods, born of huge statue and lived much longer than most. There are many accounts in history that seem erroneous with biblical characters such as Noah being 950 years old so perhaps the Sumerian and Enoch writings of eternal beings are true as the Sumerian texts suggest. The bloodline of the Anunnaki is believed to be with us still and it is suggested that this is the ruling class of today, the people who hold the gold, keeping the true past of our creation a closely guarded secret, suppressing any evidence that may reveal these facts and enlighten us.

Greek mythology is a complex tangle of demigods and wars of power describing mixed creatures of animal and man. The centaur being part man and part horse, the Minotaur with the head of a bull, Bacchus the god of wine and merriment, the keeper of woods who danced with the cherubim from the heavens with goat's legs. Although an extremely long fable of myths and legends verbally handed down through the ages, this is the period from where these stories where spawned. The Greek Apocalypse of Baruch in Greek mythology tells of the Titans, their name for the sons of Nephilim, being destructive to mankind. The gods decided that Earth was to be wiped clean to rid the giants from humanity, so the Flood was sent.

We are already today involved in an era of cloning animals. We can now 3D print organs for use in our bodies and already we can create genetically modified embryos. I am sure we will experience the horrors of such things, these are only facts told to us in the public sector. It is not too difficult to imagine a superior race of people who have conquered space travel and have surpassed our technology of today creating us, the human. If our species overcomes the desire to destroy itself our future is rapidly heading towards longer life and the introduction of computer operated body parts and the fine tuning of human perfection, although as a result, total control of the people.

A Sumerian king called Nimrod who was thought to have built the famous 'Tower of Babel' in Babylon was thought to be mythical until early 2003 when archaeologists discovered a stash of golden artefacts with trinkets and swords with written tablets connected directly to the king. It was the lost treasure of Nimrod, which had been stored in a museum in Iraq for some time. Slowly our mythical past is being shown to be fact.

Nimrod was a fierce warrior and king, one of several who reigned over Babylon and Sumur in Iraq after the deluge. It is written that Nimrod was a demigod with direct descendants from the Nephilim, the Anunnaki, who mated with genetically changed humans. There are many stories that surround the myths of giant people in these times. The giants had similar irregularities, six toes on each foot, six fingers on each hand and two sets of teeth with colossal heights ranging from 10-31 feet with great stance and strength. The giant myth is prevalent in Greek mythology also with many stories dating back to the true creation of man.

In archives dating back to the 1800s there are events of pioneering discoveries finding 12 ft tall human remains in most continents. There are over 200 separate articles on giant skeletons found around the world, also skulls with elongated craniums, sculls of a different race to us. To name a few articles that can be sourced; in 1891 in Tuson, Arizona a 12 ft. human skeleton was found with double teeth, 12 toes and 12 fingers. Also in 1931 in Lake Homboldt, Louisiana the same anomaly was found. In Turkey, one of the main stations of the gods, whole skeletons were unearthed of giant stature. In 1934 in Jubbulpore Village, Calcutta a 31 ft 6 inch giant human skeleton was unearthed and news of this circulated the planet reaching various newspapers as far as Sydney, Australia on 10 August.

In Peru a mass burial site near Cerro Colorado was found opposite an existing dig. They found elongated sculls with a cranial volume 2.5 times larger than conventional modern human skulls. Cultures from around the world drew images of their leaders having elongated skulls and huge stance. These people ruled earth in ancient times. The same we find in Egypt with images having the same shaped heads. These artefacts of the giant human skulls were on display for all to see at the time of their discovery back in the 1700s/1800s. It was big world news at the time but if you enquire now to view the evidence, your request is in vain. In Bolivia you can still view the skulls found but in many countries these artefacts are hidden from public view by the authorities. The Vatican holds a selection of elongated sculls in the depths of its catacombs but these are not available for public viewing.

On the walls of the tombs in the Valley of the Kings there are numerous hydroliths clearly showing giant sized people of 4 metres carrying huge stones next to smaller human sized people, depicting the construction of the great pyramids. It was a race of people clearly described in 'The Book of Enoch' and other reliant sources of ancient history.

The Book of Enoch, the book that was long forgotten because of its controversial log of history, plainly describes in detailed chapters, people called the Nephilim. "There were giants on the earth in those days and also after that, when the sons of the gods came in unto the daughters of men and they bear children to them, the same become mighty men which were of old, men of renown". The whole religious aspect has been distorted and corrupted. It is not one god; it is a race of superior beings of a greater stance and intelligence who have mastered the art of space travel. These gods are our creators.

Most pre-Flood ruins in South America, Egypt, Baalbek and the rest of the world were built with megalithic sized stones using a technique still unknown. They worked with quarried stone in sizes that would certainly challenge us today as 300 tons is the maximum we can quarry and move with contemporary machinery. They stacked the blocks in a system of geometry which resists earthquakes and tremors keeping the structures solid. They used no mortar between the stones but cut the geometric shaped blocks with such accuracy that they fit together without the thickness of a sheet of paper being able to be slipped between the joints. The right angles and flatness of these cuts could have only been done in such huge pieces of rock with some kind of superior ancient technology that we have no knowledge of today. This was just an era, the same as any other culture which shows up all round the world in the same time frame but built by a different race of people. These simple observations seem to be omitted and ignored in building the true history of this time. After the Flood that destroyed most of life, it is quite clear that all buildings were made of much smaller stone and mud bricks. Until you view the ruins in Baalbek, Lebanon which is mentioned in the Sumerian tablets as being the launch place of the Anunnaki space craft, you cannot comprehend the enormity of the stones used, one being the largest cut stone on earth weighing approximately 1,250 tons, and carved from the bedrock. This is not the work of our species in a timeframe when we were supposed to be hunter gatherers.

The pyramids and other megalithic ancient structures around the world are built on a global geometric grid system on key positions of energy lines or ley lines thought to extract energy from the earth, a technique lost to history. Although the Giza Pyramid is widely believed to be the burial structure for a pharaoh in Egypt, it is untrue as most of the pharaohs are buried in the Valley of the Kings some distance away from these structures. The tombs themselves are decorated with depictions of the road to the afterlife and stories of their reign with gold and trinkets to make the passage to the afterlife as comfortable as possible. But the Giza Pyramid has none of these things as it was built for another purpose. The pyramid was constructed with an estimated 250 million stone blocks, with granite inside as a natural radiator with a thick layer of limestone as an insulating liner around the outside, with a pyramidal capstone made of gold as a conductor. It has a labyrinth of tunnels unconnected with the layout of a burial chamber but more consistent with the workings of ancient technology bringing huge amounts of natural power from the earth or the sky. Many of the temples in other countries like Angkor Wot in Cambodia and Peru, South America have been rebuilt on the same sacred sites because of its global grid position. Objects found in pottery and artefacts on the site by historians only date the presence of the last civilisation that lived there, not necessarily the date of construction. Rock cannot be carbon dated so we rely on objects found and local legends to place a date on a particular site. Nickola Tesla, the true genius of the last century, produced his power dome 100 years ago in America, a tower capable of pulling millions of volts from the ionosphere free. The belief is some of these worldly structures built on energy grids were used in some form of lost technology, to produce power similar to Tesla's idea.

The famed finding of the 'Bagdad Battery' which dates back to 250 BC is a vessel used to produce electricity. It was thought to have been used for gold plating jewellery proving the technology was around in these times. In

Egyptian hieroglyphics it clearly shows the use of huge lighting filaments of some kind which still puzzles archaeologists today.

The positioning of the Giza Pyramid is accurate to one inch facing due north, an incredible feat of engineering for these times unless aided by those with superior knowledge. The three main pyramids of Giza are a geographical replica of the 'Three King's Star' in space, the constellation of Orion. There are other buildings seen from aerial shots which join up and form the whole constellation. The position of Orion's phallus is the direction in which 'The ones who came from the sky' first visited earth and the reason the pharaohs positioned the pyramids so precisely, 'As above as below', mirroring the star constellation and its shape on Earth.

There is much debate on which year the pyramids where constructed. The Giza Pyramid has ruins beneath its foundation suggesting that it was reconstructed, a new development on the site of an older structure. The Sphinx however gives us the clues to when the site was first formed. Take into consideration the precision and geometry of the pyramids. The Giza Pyramid is a mathematical replica of Earth. If you take the height and multiply by 43,222 you get the radius of the earth. If you measure the parameter of the base and multiply by 43,222 you find the equatorial circumference of the earth, it is the work of a genius. When viewing the sphinx the pharaoh's head is completely out of proportion to the body of the lion being considerably smaller. The pyramid was built accurate to one inch of true north, so why would the sphinx be disproportional? The sphinx was originally carved in limestone from one piece directly from the bedrock where it stands. The pharaoh's head is made of a quarried building stone quite clearly a different colour and in much better condition than the lion's body. In 1857 'The Stele of Revealing' was discovered between the front legs of the sphinx. It is a carving telling the story back in 3,100 BC of Pharaoh Khafra renovating the weathered sculpture carving the face of his brother on the wind torn monument. Perhaps here is where the lion gained its new identity from the head of lion to the head of a pharaoh.

Until you start applying other factual aspects and truly understand what these structures were for, your conclusion will always be vague and most definitely not based on truth. As I suggested earlier our forefathers based their life around esoteric and astrological teachings and were very much connected and influenced by the zodiac cycles and the precession of Earth. When the new star installation appeared in the March equinox, they would every 2,160 years celebrate the coming of the new era and pre-build monuments to adorn this great event. 48 BC was the beginning of the Age of Pisces with pairs of fish, the symbol of this sign, showing up in mosaics and sculptures in societies all round the world.

The Sphinx is not just a strange animal with a different head and body, it is a highly calculated piece of engineering representing the turn of an age which is also positioned geometrically for a reason. On the vernal equinox at the Age of Leo which was 10,848 BC, the sun was positioned exactly above the head of the Sphinx with the Sphinx facing due east, this mammoth structure was constructed to celebrate the dawn of the new age of Leo, as the figure of a lion. If the Sphinx was built in the period 3,500 BC as the historians believe, it would have been the sculpture of a bull representing the Age of Taurus.

The earth is a molten core of iron and nickel with a thin outer crust on which we live. Tectonic plates form the continents and over thousands of years shift, moving in different directions and coming together forming mountains and other land anomalies. The earth has an axis north to south and acts very similar to a gyroscope. The earth is halfway through its life and is starting to slow down, this causes the ends of the axis to wobble like a gyroscope. This circular wobble is known as the 'precession' which takes 2,160 years to complete one cycle. The axis points to all 12 zodiac signs, as star constellations, on its journey with each sign being called an Age like 'The Age of Aquarius'. This precession is the larger cycle of the annual zodiac signs that most of us use relating to our annual birth dates. Whilst studying the distant past these dates can be of use as many cultures used the signs in their art work and sculpture.

Although the exact dates are debated, I have used the Age of Pisces 48 BC as the starting point to calculate the dates of the Zodiac Ages as it is a time in proven history with most reference.

Aquarius: 21,11 AD – 42,72 AD

Pisces: 48 BC – 21,11 AD

Aries: 2,208 BC – 48 BC

Taurus: 4,368 BC – 2,208 BC

Gemini: 6,528 BC – 4,368 BC

Cancer: 8,688 BC – 6,528 BC

Leo: 10,848 BC – 8688 BC

Virgo: 13,008 BC – 10,848 BC

Libra: 15,168 BC – 13,008 BC

Scorpio: 17,328 BC – 15,168 BC

Sagittarius: 19,488 BC – 17,328 BC

Capricorn: 21,648 BC – 19,488 BC

If the calendar started with Leo with the building of the Sphinx in 10,848 BC this gives a precise year to work with fitting in the other sections of lost history. The coming Age of Aquarius has many aspects in common with the end of other similar calendars made by other cultures like the Mayans, so the precession zodiac calendar may well have commenced with the Age of Capricorn in 21,648 BC making Aquarius the last Age in the cycle of 12 signs, putting the Sumerian texts and true Egyptian King Ship in place.

THE FATHER OF OCCULTISM AND WORSHIP OF BAPHOMET

KING SOLOMON 970BC

Solomon the King of Israel was the most important keystone in history to understanding the darker side of things and what is really going on in this world. Many brotherhoods and secret societies use the teachings of Solomon as the basis and beginning of their cult. It is written that he was the richest man on earth boasting 700 wives and 300 concubines which is still practised in Arabia today to show their status. His wealth although contrary to belief came from mining copper not gold in the nearby town of Khirbet en Nahas near the 'Dead sea' rift valley. Solomon built the first temple in Jerusalem by divine order making him the king and prophet of the Jewish followers of the old Hebrew religion with the construction of the temple 'The Holy of Holies'. He had strong contacts with Egypt the governing power of that region at the time with the fabled queen of Sheba visit bringing him gifts of gold and spices. Solomon was known as the all wise and all-knowing king at the start with his knowledge and philosophy and ability to govern the people fairly.

Solomon was the keeper of the 'Ark of the Covenant' the most important and sought-after piece of ancient treasure searched for by many to this day. The Ark is a box measuring 2.5 cubits x 1.5 cubits x 1.5 cubits high, (a cubit being 45.72cm) It is carried by two fixed poles either side of the Ark with a 'mercy seat' positioned on top. Two cherubim are positioned at both ends of the ark with their wings touching each other in the middle of the mercy seat. The whole construction is made of shitm wood/Acacia, from the Middle East and is layered with solid gold. Solomon was the king of the Jews and he built the temple to house the Ark as the keeper of the Ark rules the world. Inside the Ark were kept the ten commandment stones, the Rod of Aaron and a vessel of Manna, the hallucinogen bread made of purified gold. The Ark is an earthly copy of the seat from which the gods rule their kingdom in space. Moses was told to build the Ark through divine instruction by the gods whilst on Mount Sinai. The story is told that the gods will return and rule earth once more, from the Mount, in a new temple which is still to be built, using the Ark of the Covenant as their throne. This is why the Temple Mount or 'Holy of Holies' is the most important piece of real estate in the world and causes so much carnage. When the temple was destroyed in 587 BC by the Romans, the Ark was thought to have been hidden in the mountains so as not to be stolen and has never been discovered since that time.

It is written that Solomon had the wisdom and knowledge of calling up spirits to use their power for worldly gain. He was chosen by the gods to rule Israel and at first he was loyal and followed his divine instruction. Later it is thought through the influence of some of his concubines from other cultures, he changed his allegiance and started to worship idols, one being Molech the Ammonite god where child sacrifice was first implied as offerings to the Gods. The early pagan worship was for the planet Saturn or Satan from which the Pentagon sign originally started, this very god, adopted the symbol of the anti-Christ which is the forefront of contemporary cult worship. The belief that god is the devil and the devil is god is the controversial statement that arises in many cults which believe and follow the teachings of Solomon. The devil or the snake in the Garden of Eden who spoke to Eve said that if we eat the apple of truth, you yourself will become a God in our own right not ruled by a superior. The cults believe the snake tells the truth and saves us from the dark. A secret ring with the sign of the Jewish pentagon is one of the artefacts believed to have been used by Solomon to summon the demons and which people still search for today.

The devil himself has never written a book so most writings are biased. The devil and hell are fabricated by the Roman Catholic Church as a place for sinners when you die. Our ancestors, before commercial religion, believed we all went to a place called Shail, a place that all humans went to, good or bad, or later 'Nirvana' believed in by the Vikings. So the devil is manmade, although if we are to discuss the goods and Evils of the spirit world, then this is a different matter.

THE ORIGINS OF CONTEMPORARY CULTS

Albert Pike was one of the true fathers of occultism, a member of the Ku Klux Klan and a leading figure in world domination. He was born in 1809 in Boston USA. He studied at Harvard, and later served as a Brigadier-General in the Confederate Army. After the Civil War Pike was found guilty of treason and jailed but later pardoned by fellow Freemason President Andrew Johnson on 22 April 1866 - he was in the club.

Pike was said to be a genius, mastering 16 different languages and writing books on philosophy and humanitarianism. He was also a philanthropist and an active lawyer. He soon scaled the degrees in the Masonic Order and become a 33rd Degree Mason. He was one of the founding fathers, and head of the Ancient Scottish Rite of Freemasonry, being the Grand Commander of North American Masonic Lodge. He retained that position until his death in 1891 and also held a position in the Knights of the Ku Klux Klan and was Grand Master of the Sovereign Council of Wisdom.

Albert Pike describes in his books the world network of establishing and bringing about the New World Order, with the aim of enforced control of mankind, events that would lead to global financial control and the bringing forth of the three world wars, of which one is still to be played out. It is written and echoed in the writings of Pike that he played a huge part in the preparation for the First World Wars and the French Revolution. The person who wrote the blueprint for the 'New world Order' acting alongside the founders of the Illuminati, Albert Pike is the only Confederate Generals with a statue on federal property in Washington DC, being honoured not as a lawyer, but as Southern Regional Leader of the Scottish Rite of Freemasonry. In 1871, Pike published the Masonic handbook named 'Morals and Dogma of the Ancient and Accepted Scottish Rite of Freemasonry' explaining all these facts.

"Lucifer is God and unfortunately Adonay is also God for eternal Law, there is no light without shade, no beauty without ugliness, no white without black being necessary for light to serve as its foil." Albert Pike (Ref.Sec.5)

THE WICKEDEST MAN ON EARTH

Although Albert pike lead the way in the 1800s a new image of occultism revealed itself in the form of a man called Alistair Crowley with the media naming him the 'wickedest man on earth'. Mr Crowley was a member of the 'Golden Dawn' cult which practised Black magic and attracted many famous elitists and society moguls. He was an extremist stating that it matters not what you do as long as it is strong. He preached his own philosophy on religion and rule which states 'Do what though wilt'; this was the entirety of his law. After declaring himself 'the beast 666' and the death of Christianity, his relationship with the Golden Dawn cult broke down suggesting they were only playing at Black Magic and he would set up his own cult taking the art of demonic worship to the extremes. Many of the world's cults today are based on the teachings of King Solomon who worshipped the idol of Baphomet.

He chose a suitable ritual house near the banks of Lochness, Scotland where the building still stands but many still today choose not to cross its path. He undertook a ritual that takes six months to complete involving isolation and ritual chant. This ancient practice is called 'The Abra Mellen' an extremely dangerous procedure beckoning the Devil into our realm from another dimension with the goal of using its power for worldly gain and control. In King Solomon's time during the worship of the God Baphomet, blood sacrifice was an accepted procedure to please their gods and it is still used today around the world in many different cultures.

The origin of the name Baphomet is a combination of two Greek words 'baphe' and 'metis' meaning 'absorption of knowledge.' The 'Goat of Mendes' or the Black Goat, is one of the symbols of Freemasonry. The goat represents fertility and symbol of the Magnum Opus of alchemy.

In 1919 Crowley took some of his members and set up his own cult in Cefalu Sicily which he called 'The Abbey of Thelma'. He performed with his wife and other followers extreme sexual depravity involving animal and human participation in the worship of Satan. In 1920 the leader of

Italy, Mussolini, condemned the Abbey and deported the whole cult. The derelict building still stands today with murals that Alistair painted during his stay with the locals declaring it a place of evil. He was an educated man high in the ranks of freemasonry and other cults but believed and stood against any rule or compromise over man.

He influenced a new wave of cult worship in the 60s with the evolution of the drug and music scene making the worship of the devil popular with his teachings of 'do as thou wilt' and anti-control of the masses. The pop group The Beatles put his face on the front cover of their album 'Sgt Pepper's Lonely Hearts Club Band' and many smaller cult groups soon emerged with rebellious undertones with people like Charles Manson following the trend.

THE TIMELINE OF HUMANITY

Take into consideration that when talking in billions of years scientific evidence is only as good as the day it was written. These are periods of time estimated by our archaeologists and historians to the best of their knowledge and capabilities using today's dating systems. In the future when technology advances these dates will alter.

We are only just scratching the surface of what really happened thousands of years ago, most of which is submersed below the sea with unexplored areas of the world such as the polar caps which have had minimal exploration. Future excavations will unravel and secure the hidden truth of our past.

13.7 billion years ago the 'Big Bang Theory', the start of the universe and everything according to mainstream scientists. But what made the first atoms in the first place and what is the exploding universe expanding into, more space and where did that come from, another explosion? And so the question still remains.

4.6 billion years ago the Earth was formed along with our moon allowing each other through the magnetic field caused by their iron and nickel core, to harmonize and generate a future living planet.

4.5 billion years ago the world was a molten spherical mass of elements, Hydrogen, carbon, oxygen and nitrogen the very building blocks of life, spinning at a high resolution equating to six hour days.

4.1 billion years ago the atmosphere on Mars which originally sustained life gradually depleted rendering the surface uninhabitable by unknown phenomena leaving the planet desolate and lifeless on the surface.

850 - 635 million years ago the seas of our Earth were frozen along with most of the land mass.

570 million years ago the first bacteria, corals, trilobites and shellfish were beginning to form and grow. It is believed that a meteor crashed into the earth and deposited bacteria which began the first foundation of life.

438 million years ago the first land masses with plant and vegetation emerged.

400 million years ago oxidation was well underway which started to cause steam and eventually rain clouds, so the cycle begun. Freshwater lakes and seas started to evolve.

360 million years ago swamps and forests started to develop with signs of reptiles and insects.

350 million years ago the start of the Jurassic Period.

250 million years ago the end of most large mammals and extinction of many species, thought to be a meteor hitting Earth near Mexico rendering the planet's atmosphere heavily polluted, unfit for vegetative growth and challenging for all creatures to survive.

65 million years ago apes and primates started to evolve, the first of our ancestors, early man, the first use of flint tools.

37 million years ago the North African Sahara Desert was under water, today showing fossils of whales and small sea creatures in abundance under the sand.

20 million years ago the North African region was tropical swamp land unlike the desert we know today.

15 million years ago Antarctica was ice free with a warm climate.

1.8 million years ago an ice age occurred depopulating the world by an estimated 70 % of all creatures.

780,000 years ago the magnetic pole reversal (which happens approximately every 200,000 years on average) where the magnetic north and south magnetic poles reverse causing various difficulties for wild life navigation and possible destructive sea variations.

450,000 years ago Anunnaki 'Those who from the heavens came' people from another orbiting planet came to our earth and genetically modified the Homo-sapiens for slavery, used for mining gold, according to the story written on clay tablets found in Iraq, also written in the Book of Enoch and Papyrus papers.

160,000 years ago the oldest skull to date representing the human form was found in Ethiopia putting our species back to this date.

70,000 years ago Aborigines in Australia and New Zealand have been recorded present by fossil remains. One of the longest surviving groups of humans on earth.

41,000 years ago on the coast of Turkey in some of the oldest caves were found the first examples of creative art being made as well as hunting tools.

36,000 years ago the true start of the Egyptian dynasty, publicly debated but written and carved on the walls of Egypt.

25,000 years ago remains of red haired elongated skulls and giant-sized skeletons from this period have been found, a different species to man and unknown origin.

21,648 BC – 19,488 BC The Age of Capricorn. The start of a complex calendar using the knowledge and positioning of the stars, the 2,160 year precession of the axis of the globe showing the twelve signs of the Zodiac, suggesting the rulers of humankind at this time, had knowledge of our galaxy.

19,488 BC – 17,328 BC The Age of Sagittarius.

19,128 BC The Age of Ophiuchusn is the secret sign unknown to most positioned between Sagittarius and Scorpio. It is the 13th star sign which aligns with the 'Dark Rift' in the star constellations known as the serpent holder.

17,328 BC – 15,168 BC The Age of Scorpio.

15,168 BC – 13,008 BC The Age of Libra.

14,400 BC The water table was at its lowest point at this time meaning many of the continental land masses were connected, unlike today where we are living on the peaks.

13,008 BC – 10,848 BC The Age of Virgo.

10,848 – 8,688 BC The Age of Leo. Connected to the world's precession cycle showing the true era in which the construction of the great Sphinx in Egypt was constructed before the Flood.

10,848 BC The sphinx was built for the Spring Equinox in 10,848 BC to celebrate the bringing in of a new Zodiac Age. The Great Flood must have happened after the construction of the Sphinx, as water erosion is clear to see on the base of the monument today in Egypt, in a place that has been desert for thousands of years.

10,000 BC Gobeki Tepe is one of the oldest surviving relics from before the flood in the form of what is believed to be a place of worship, an astral temple. Some of the oldest remains on earth were found in Turkey going back to this date.

9,600 BC The end of the megalithic construction techniques of huge monumental structures. The end of a great civilisation, wiped out by the flood, taking their building technique of mammoth stone construction to the grave.

9,600 BC The historic event of the 'Great flood', the deluge that wiped the earth clean of most living things and left carnage in its wake. This event has been documented by all major civilisations leaving wall paintings and papyrus writings all round the world; the story of Noah. The exact date of the flood is vague but archaeological evidence leans towards the period of 9,600 and 10,000 BC. Plato later wrote that this was the time when Atlantis was destroyed and swallowed by the ocean believed to be near the Hercules gates of Gibraltar where many other cities were destroyed. Plato also gave this date for the deluge. Although we understand a worldwide tsunami occurred of some kind, not all corners of the world would have been affected. The Aborigines of Australia believe that their ancestry goes back unbroken for 70,000 years.

8,700 BC In Iraq, copper pendants were found in burial graves dating back well before the alleged Copper Age of around 4,500 BC. Copper was first recorded in Britain at around 2,500 BC.

8,688 BC – 6,528 BC The Age of Cancer. The time our forefathers who survived the great flood started to regroup and form new towns and settlements. Archaeological evidence suggests that Mesopotamia and the Arab states was the region that man reformed after the deluge.

8,000 BC The birth of the Druid religion, the first signs archaeologically of people worshipping the sun.

7,900 BC Proven archaeological evidence found in Kuwait of human remains and habitation dating back to 7,900 BC.

6,528 BC – 4,368 BC The Age of Gemini.

5,000 BC Eriden one of the first cities in Mesopotamia recorded in Ancient history as being in existence.

4,368 BC – 2,208 BC The age of Taurus.

4,100 BC The Anunnaki, the creators of man, were believed to have left Earth, according to the Mesopotamian tablets, stating that they will return in the Age of Aquarius. It is thought that they departed from Baalbek Lebanon, where mammoth megalithic stones weighing hundreds of tons still lay today.

4,004 BC The date given by the Catholic Church and the Archbishop of Dublin for the start of the universe, the creation of man and all things by their god. (If the Genesis of the bible is to hold any credence at all, it is a metaphor describing the genetic creation of man and women by the Anunnaki, not the start and creation of the Universe and all things).

3,761 BC The Hebrew Jewish start date of the creation of Earth and the start of the Universe.

3,750 BC – 4,250 BC The 'Carnac' astrological stone calendar was made in Brittany, France.

3,100 BC Pharaoh Menes, The first Egyptian pharaoh as we are taught, before the flood, although this is untrue, the lineage of the pharaohs goes much further back according to the Sumerian tablets.

2,948 BC The construction of Solomon's Temple, the great King and philosopher, the wealthiest man on earth of his time, holder of the 'Ark of the Covenant' and the secret ring of the underworld. Worshipper of Molech the Ammonite God where child sacrifice was first associated with religious Pagan rituals.

2,700 – 2,500 BC The reign of Gilgamesh the king of Uruk in Mesopotamia, thought to be the last demigod ruling on earth, carrying the blood line of the Anunnaki.

2,700 BC The start of the Bronze Age. With the discovery of tin in China and Britain we discovered the formula of mixing 5% tin with copper producing bronze, a much harder and lighter metal capable of holding a sharp edge. This started a new age of machinery and tools.

2,480 BC The death of the Egyptian Pharaoh Khafra.

2,348 BC The Bible's date for the 'Great Flood' and the story of Noah.

2,208 BC – 48 BC The age of Aries.

2,167 BC Nimrod the king and ruler of Babylon who was thought to have built the great tower of Babel dies in this year. Nimrod the founder of paganism was born December 25th. This date is the birth of the new sun astrologically at the end of each year, celebrated in pagan worship in Babylon but later used deceptively by the Catholic Church as a civic holiday to represent the birth of Christ in 350 AD by Pope Julius. The pagan translation 'Dies natalis solis inicti' means 'the birthday of the unconquered sun'

Nimrod, the grandson of Noah was believed to be a demigod, his mother and wife being the same person, Semiramis, was also known as Ishtar or Isis. Nimrod is also known in Egypt as Osiris the sun god. A few years after his death, Semiramis his wife declared that the spirit of Nimrod had caused the pregnancy and that Horus, her new born son, was the reincarnation of Nimrod himself.

2,023 BC The destruction of the great city of Sumur which was caused by a war between Marduk and Henlow, the blood line of the Anunnaki according to the Sumerian tablets.

2,023 BC Abraham the Jewish prophet dies leaving his son Isaac.

2,000 BC Stonehenge, the famous stone calendar is estimated to have been built in Salisbury, Britain.

1,917 BC The city of Sodom and Gomorrah was destroyed which was the last recorded violent act of the Anunnaki Gods. The cities ruins are located south of the Dead Sea which are still being excavated today.

1,800 BC The period thought to be the beginning of the Mayan civilisation.

1,792 BC – 1,750 BC The Era of King Hammurabi ruling Babylon.

1,473 – 1,425 BC King Thutmose 4th ruled Egypt.

1,391 BC – 1,271 BC The birth and life span of Moses according to the Torah and Jewish belief.

1,332 BC – 1,323 BC Tutankhamun ruled the empire of Egypt within this period.

1,323 BC – 1,279 BC Pharaoh Seti rules over Egypt.

1,312 BC – 1,280 BC The Torah, the bible of the Hebrew Jews was believed to have been written in these times although the true authors are debated. The Christians believe they were made by Moses by divine instruction although the Jews believe it to be the workings of Abraham.

1,292 BC – 1,290 BC Rameses I ruled over Egypt.

970 BC – 931 BC The great King Solomon ruled Israel from the temple in Jerusalem, on the Holy of Holies Mount. No factual evidence has ever been found of Solomon's temple but it is one of the most documented pieces of History, the start of divine Israel.

800 BC The Iron Age, a useful element found by humanity which changed our capabilities of building and agriculture, first used in Europe and china and later found its way to Britannia.

722 BC The Assyrians become the strongest empire in Iraq and surrounding regions.

627 BC The famous Library of Syria founded by Ashham Bontipal was recorded of being in existence. Later it was destroyed with many old scripts of our true history lost.

623 BC – 544 BC Lord Buddha or Gautama Buddha was born (although exact dates are vague) who preached that you yourselves are your own saviour, heralding the start of the finest peace-loving religion known to man. A way of self-enlightenment and conducting life in harmony with nature and fellow man, still practised today. There is no god to answer to; you are reborn after death being reincarnated into a new body. Until you reach enlightenment, you will return to earth in a cycle of lives, when enlightenment is reached you ascend to heaven. (If all people of the world practised his philosophy, the world would be a better place).

605 BC - 562 BC The death of King Nebuchadnezzar II who ruled the City of Babylon (Babylon translated means 'Gate of the Gods') referring to the great tower of Babel built to talk with the Gods.

587 BC King David's Temple in Jerusalem was burnt to the ground and pillaged of all its gold and perhaps the Ark of the Covenant by King Nebuchadnezzar the Babylonian king. The Ark has never been seen since this date but many have tried to find it. The keeper of the Ark of the Covenant is said to have access to all worldly power and wealth.

551 BC - 479 BC The birth of Confucius or Kong Qui the Chinese Philosopher who gave the Chinese wisdom and a moral code of living in harmony and respect for fellow man.

539 BC The Babylonian city was taken over by the Persians and the Jews which were enslaved were allowed back to Jerusalem.

509 BC The republic of Rome was founded in Constantinople, today called Istanbul in Turkey.

500 BC – 580 BC Pythagoras entered history and after 80 years died in Greece leaving the world a better place with his philosophy and the basic building blocks of geometry.

470 - 360 BC Democritus was one of the first philosophers to develop 'atomic theory'. Democritus believed all matter consisted of one substance called prime matter. He called the smallest unit of prime matter atoms.

460 BC – 430 BC Hippocrates was born in Greece, the origin of the saying 'Hippocratic Oath' still used today in law and doctrine.

428 BC - 384 BC Plato was born giving mankind insight into philosophy and starting the first university north of Athens Greece, he was also the writer who mentioned the existence of Atlantis.

399 BC - 470 BC Socrates the philosopher was born in Athens, Greece. He is best known for his 'Socratic Method' on which the western world based its foundations of philosophy and logic. He was eventually accused by the Greek courts of heresy and charged with impiety and the corruption of youth. His philosophies undermined the teachings of the church and he was seen as a threat to the closed religious dogma, he was sentenced to death by lethal injection.

384 BC - 322 BC The famous philosopher Aristotle was born and gave the world insight into many controversial things declaring "The brain exists merely to cool the blood of the body not the process of thinking", subscribing to the belief of a conscious soul separate to the body.

374 BC King Herod built a new temple in Jerusalem in the same position as the ruins of Solomon's temple.

339 BC - 263 BC Eusebius of Caesarea a respected Roman historian with many reliable factual records of his time, died in Israel.

322 BC Alexander the Great conquered Egypt becoming king and ruler.

330 BC – 275 BC Euclid or also known as Eukleides the famous teacher who carried on from Aristotle teaching geometry and construction angles.

300 BC The City of Troy south west of Turkey was established; thought to have been myth until recently when the ruins were discovered, part of the Mediterranean ancient world.

255 BC The great Alexandria Library was established, famed to be the finest collection of ancient literature of all time until it was destroyed eventually by the Roman invasion of Egypt depriving future generations of the previous knowledge of our true origin.

250 BC The 'Baghdad battery' which was unearthed in Khujutrabu, Baghdad, dates back to 250 BC. A clay vessel which produces electricity thought to be used for gold plating, with the anodes and cathodes still in place, putting the invention of electricity well before Nikola Tesla.

48 BC – 21, 11 AD The Age of Pisces.

30 BC – 69 BC Cleopatra the Queen of Egypt makes the last stand in the dynasty of Egyptian ruling Kings, the Empire falls.

30 BC The end of the Egyptian empire, taken by the Romans led by Augustus Caesar ruled by Cleopatra who took her own life using the bite of a snake, thought to be myth until the discovery of the city of Alexandria under the ocean off the coast of Egypt, still being excavated today.

The year 1 AD The Birth of Christ the Christian Prophet who was killed by the Jews, giving birth to Monotheism, the worship of one God. The actual dates are debated

70 AD August 29th, the Romans burnt down the second temple on the Holy Mount in Jerusalem and took control of the city led by Emperor Titus accompanied by Tiberius the Second General.

132 AD The Romans completely levelled Jerusalem and built a new city called 'Aelia Capitolina' to rid the city of any remaining Jews.

325 AD Constantine the Emperor of Rome published the first bible made up of several plagiarised texts copied from Egyptian scripts and pieces from the book of Enoch to suit his needs to form a believable religion to rule and suppress the masses under the hood of 'The Roman Catholic Church'.

400 AD In the southern region of Mexico the area now known as Cancun, showers of meteors hit the earth leaving huge holes still visible today causing mass evacuation of this area.

509 AD The city of Rome was made a republic after overthrowing King Lucius Tarquinius.

637 AD - 1099 AD The Muslim religion held the sacred mount in Jerusalem.

1042 AD – 1066 AD Edward the Confessor was the last Anglo-Saxon king of England until his death in January 1066 AD. King Harold Godwinson II inherited the crown for a short period until his demise 9 months later in the 'Battle of Hastings' against William the Conqueror.

1099 AD The Christians took back the holy mount in Jerusalem by force from the Muslims, the sacred place of Solomon's Temple and the believed landing place of our true makers the Anunnaki.

1120 AD 'The Knights Templar' held power over the Jerusalem mount and conducted excavations whilst controlling passage for the Christian pilgrims. The quest for finding the 'Ark of the Covenant' and the secrets of the Holy Grail, 'the lost knowledge'.

1162 AD The reign of Genghis Khan, the Mongolian slaughter of the Middle East.

1187 AD The Knights Templar lost the sacred mount back to the Muslims in the battle of 'Hattin' to the Sultan Saladin.

1215 AD The Magna Carta. The Magna Carta (Great Charter) was signed by King John, the king Of England announcing that all people including the King would abide by the English law of the land and guaranteed the rights of the individual person against the sole wish of the Crown.

1274 – 1329 AD The life of Robert the Bruce famous for his Scottish interaction in the war against England.

1291 AD The Knights Templar left the Holy Land, the quest was won.

1345 AD The beginning of the Aztec tribes in Mexico.

1347 – 1351 AD The 'Black Death' plague hit Europe and laid to death an estimated 20 million people which was half of the population at the time.

1492 AD Christopher Columbus was the man who first started to colonise and pillage North America but not the first to discover it. The Vikings in the 10th Century and the Chinese shortly after, first made their mark on discovering the lands.

1475 AD The birth of Copernicus, a well-known astrologer and artist being remembered mostly for his idea that all planets rotate round the sun in our galaxy not round the earth, which was previously thought.

1490 AD Roslyn Chapel in Scotland UK was built by the Knights Templar where some Knights were laid to rest and can still be seen to this day.

1491 – 1547 Henry VIII. The reign of King Henry VIII in Great Britain was from 1509 AD until his death in 1547 AD, succeeding his father Henry VII.

1535 – 1542 Between 1535-1542 Wales become subject to British Law whilst under the kingship of Henry V11 becoming an equal part of the 'Kingdom of England'. Following the hereditary position gained by King James V1, the King of England ruled from 1603 AD.

1535 A catastrophic event affected the whole world leaving the atmosphere and skies darkened with polluted air, blocking the sun. It lasted for twenty years stunting the growth of trees and vegetation, causing floods but little rain. It caused plagues and starvation for many people. It was thought to be caused by the Krakatoa volcano erupting.

1542 Leonardo Da Vinci was born leaving clues and hidden signs in his works of art to alert future generations of events to come. The finest artist and inventor of his time.

1547 The Bubonic Plague which wiped out thousands of European and English people, thought to be connected to the Krakatoa eruption in 1535 AD.

1564 – 1642 Galileo the Italian born physicist and astronomer was famed for his discovery of the four Moons of Jupiter and also for the invention of the telescope.

1582 The beginning of the Gregorian Calendar, brought into use in by Pope Gregory in October 1582, using AD 'Anno Domini' the medieval Latin translation meaning 'In the year of the Lord' not the misunderstood 'After death' as many use.

1603 Union of the Crowns. King James VI ruled England, Scotland and Wales as one King following the death of Queen Elizabeth leaving no heir to the throne.

1608 Galileo was said to have invented the first telescope although Hans Lippershey tried to obtain the first patent in 1608 on September 25.

1611 The King James Bible, the New Testament, came in to circulation, the first complete English translation.

1643 – 1727 Isaac Newton was born January 4, 1643. He was a physicist and mathematician who developed the principles of modern physics, including the laws of motion, and is credited as one of the great minds of the 17th Century. In 1687 he published his most acclaimed work, 'Mathematical Principles of Natural Philosophy' which has been called the single most influential book on physics. In 1705 he was knighted by Queen Anne of England making him Sir Isaac Newton.

1665 The great plague of London killed an estimated 100,000 people, one in every three of the populace; this was reported by the scribe of the time Samuel Pepys.

1688 The Revolution of England. Known as 'The Glorious Revolution' of England, the revolution was the overthrow of King James II (who wished Roman Catholicism reinstated), by a union of Parliamentarians, banning any Catholics from inheriting the throne. Finally ending the brutal influence of the Roman Catholic Church. The Dutch stadtholder, William III, Prince of Orange, married Mary II and they become king and Queen of England and Ireland.

1707 On the 1 May Great Britain was founded as a nation with the first parliament rule set up as a democracy, finishing sole rule by dictatorship of the Crown.

1712 The first steam engine was designed by a British inventor Thomas Newcomen which started the steam revolution.

1717 The official start of the Masonic Freemasons lodge in Queen Street, London UK. (One of the first members was Frederick, Prince of Wales)

1776 Adam Weishaupt started the controversial Bavarian 'Illuminati' cult.

1752 Great Britain joined the Gregorian calendar resetting their calendar accordingly, later setting the Worlds clocks to 'Greenwich Mean Time'.

1776 The 4 July 1776 is the Day of Independence for the American people after defeating the English on American soil.

1776 The birth of Napoleon. He later led the French army along with archaeologists to conquer Egypt and discover the hidden truths; he was a member of the Freemason fraternity.

1801 Great Britain and Ireland merged on 1 January 1801 to become part of 'The United Kingdom of Great Britain'

1815 On June 18 1885 the Battle of Waterloo commenced. Also the start of the Rothschild family dynasty investing in Wars and nobility for profit.

1833 The 'Skull and Bones' a controversial secret society and cult was founded in 1833 in the town of Yale USA.

1833 The end of black slavery in Great Britain with the 'Slavery Abolition Act 1833'.

1849 Sir Austen Henry Layard found the most significant piece of human history whilst excavating the 'Nineveh ruins', Iraq. 22,000 clay tablets were found written in 'Cuneiform', a type of ancient writing. They told the history of the days in the Sumerian times telling the story of the Anunnaki coming to earth from the sky and ruling over the world, engineering us by genetics to suit their needs and purpose. Later translated by Zachariah Sitchin and carbon dated back to 4,000 BC.

1855 Greenwich Mean Time was established by the inventor and engineer Sandford Fleming setting the world's time to order.

1859 Charles Darwin published his book on evolution.

1861 – 1865 American Civil War 1861-1865.

1865 President Lincoln of the United States of America was assassinated April 14 1865.

1868 the American congress created a corporate Government for the District of Columbia 'The Corporation of America' which is a privately owned company. This allows the corporation to operate outside of the original constitution of the United States.

1872 The 'Bohemian Grove' was founded in California USA, the controversial elitist club with members ranging from American Congress, Republican Presidents and Bankers that hold satanic worship rituals round a huge 40ft high wooden idol of the all-knowing owl in July of each year.

1876 The 'patent' of the first working 4 stroke combustion engine was produced and designed by Nicolaus Otto alongside Gottlieb Daimler, changing the way we lived forever.

1888 Helena Blavatsky the world famous psychic and co-founder of the 'Sophical Society' published her world view in a publication called 'The Secret Doctrine'. Manly P. Hall's review was: 'The secret doctrine' assumes the dignity of a scripture, for in its pages eternal mysteries are clothed in ancient and modern terms and to those who have eyes to see, the ageless wisdom is revealed.

1893 The first gasoline car was invented by Karl Benz in 1885 in Mannheim. The first car in Britain was in 1895.

1895 The first radio was invented by Guglielmo Marconi the Italian inventor, although Nikola Tesla had already demonstrated wireless radio in St Louis, Missouri in 1893.

1898 The Spanish American War 1898.

1908 England found oil in Masjid Suleiman, Iran, which started the industrial revolution.

1914 World War I 1914-1918.The first world war in recorded history with Britain, France, Russia, Italy and USA fighting against Germany, Austria, Hungry, Ottoman empire and Bulgaria.

1917 Hitler joined the ranks of history, an eccentric anti-Zionist dictator who believed he was descended from the Aryan race. He served in the first world and went on to try and eradicate the world of the Zionist Jews, leading Germany in the II World War.

1917 The Balfour Declaration, a document issued on 2 November to the Zionist Lord Rothschild from the British government during World War I, announcing support for the establishment of a 'National home for the Jewish people' in Palestine. A contract to hand over Palestine for aid given in the First World War by the American armies.

1921 The Council on Foreign Relations was established.

1923 Herbert Weld Blundel discovered the 'Kingship Prism' which proved the existence of kingships well before the Great flood.

1926 The television was invented by the Scottish inventor John Logie Baird in 1926. The first public viewing was in Selfridges, London and was on sale by 1934.

1939 – 1945 World War II 1939-1945. England and Germany went to war which soon escalated in a world war. The United States entered the war in 1941, after Japan's attack on Pearl Harbour. Germany surrendered in 1945, and Japan surrendered later that year, after the U.S. dropped the atomic bomb on the cities of Hiroshima and Nagasaki.

1945 The first trial of the nuclear bomb was tested in Alamogordo, New Mexico by the Americans. The inventor Robert Oppenheimer stated "I have become death the destroyer of worlds".

1946 The Dead Sea Scrolls, a part of the old Hebrew bible was found in 'Wadi Qumran' near the Dead Sea in an old pottery vessel showing the corruption of truth within the contemporary teachings of Catholic and Christian Religion.

1954 The 'Bilderberg Group' was founded in this year, a selection of Globalists and Capitalists who meet once a year to indulge in ancient ceremonies, dating back to King Solomon, and discuss the ordering and control of the world's finance and masses, one of the world's most controversial ruling organisations.

1961 – 1973 The Vietnam War. North Vietnam invaded non-communist South Vietnam in an attempt to unify the country and impose communist rule. The United States joined South Vietnam against the raid in 1961 ending in a ten year battle killing thousands of innocent people.

1965 The Dominican Republic War. In America 1965 President Lyndon Johnson sent troops to eliminate the uprising in the Dominican Republic.

1969 The human race puts the first man on the moon led by the American team of astronauts Neil Armstrong and Edwin Aldrin on July 20 1969.

1979 – 1990 Margaret Thatcher became the leader of the Conservative Party on 28 November 1979 in Great Britain leaving a huge void in the nation's staple industries.

1977 Computers were first available to the public in England starting the biggest technical revolution of mankind so far.

1983 The Grenada War. President Reagan ordered the invasion of the Caribbean nation of Grenada to overthrow its Marxist government, which had close ties with Cuba.

1989 The Panama War. The United States invasion of Panama code named 'Operation Just Cause' during the administration of President George H W Bush.

1991 George Herbert Walker Bush made the famous public speech in America announcing the 'New World Order', the unification of all countries and the rule of the earth by one private group and dictatorship, the declaration of world control and the end of human freedom.

1991 The Gulf War 1991. America and England eliminated the Iraqi dictator Saddam Husain and brought the country to its knees.

1993 The 'Tel Dan' stele discovered by Gila Cook in 1993 refers to the Kings of Israel and the house of David confirming the dates and existence of Solomon's Temple.

1993 The Somalia War. America attempted to restore order to Somalia.

1994 - 1995 The Bosnian War. During the Bosnian Civil War the U.S. became a part of NATO'S peacekeeping force in the region.

1998 – 1999 The Kosovo War in Europe. The ethnic Albanians opposed the ethnic Serbians and the Government of Yugoslavia. The bombing of Yugoslavia was the 'North Atlantic Organization', a military operation which ended in peace.

2001 The 911 Twin Tower attack in America. On 11 September 2001 America was attacked by terrorists destroying the 'New York trade centre', twin tower buildings. The attack was orchestrated according to the American government by terrorists connected to Osama Bin Laden.

2001 - 2004 Global War on Terror 2001. After the 911 incident President George Bush Jr launched the Global War on Terrorism. America begun bombing Afghanistan following the 911 incident in New York aided By Britain, although against the wish of the British people.

2029 The most contemporary concern and threat to the human race apart from self-destruction due to the ruling class, is the asteroid heading towards earth in 2029 called Apophis on April 13, weighing in at an estimated 27 million tons.

2111 AD – 4271 AD The Age of Aquarius.

CHAPTER 2

THE SIX HEADS OF THE DRAGON

THE JEWISH STORY

The Jewish religion is one of the oldest continuous belief systems in human history since 'The Great Flood' evolving from their story of Abraham and Moses, two of their first prophets. Much of the world's problems are caused by this fable of god, although most religions believe in the same guy. From the beginning, in short, the Jews were travelling people who had no land of their own, people who lived in tabernacles, tents, who roamed in the regions of Mesopotamia (today's Iraq) in the desert trading and herding goats. Their religion the same as most of the world at this time was pagan, worshipping different idols until Moses, later declared the Jewish Prophet, had what he described as divine contact with the one true god. Around 3,000 BC on Mount Sinai in Arabia (not Egypt) the alleged god gave Moses rules and regulations to live by which were later called 'The five books of the Hebrew Bible' known as the Tanakh, based on the Ten Commandments and other teachings. These events started the beginning of the one god monotheism movement. The bloodline of the Jewish religion, those who have been selected to live with god, were the descendants of Jacob's sons.

The Hebrews or Jews handed down the oral doctrine through their Rabbis, the teachings of the Talmud, the teachings of God to Abraham. The Talmud in simple terms is an ongoing encyclopaedia if you will, explaining the true meaning of the Torah, their bible, Talmud meaning 'Study of the Torah'. The Rabbi relate to the Torah as a metaphor and the Talmud shows how to interpret the metaphor in each story, so without the Talmud the Torah would be misunderstood, exactly the same as the Christian bible, metaphoric not fact. The leading Rabbis add to the Torah as years go by with new contemporary interpretations as an everlasting series of books keeping the history of Jewish religion intact.

Rabbi Judha Hanasy wrote the 'Mishna' which was the first writing of the oral teachings which makes up the first volume of the Talmud, thought to have been finished in 220 AD. It is an understanding of the ancient teachings and rituals used by the Jews as rules to live by and the teachings of their god.

The Jews have been hated and persecuted for 2,000 years, why? Jesus being Jewish himself who was named 'The King of the Jews' accused the Zionist Jewish leaders of manipulating the truth and usurping the message of the patriarchs and prophets of the Old Testament. He said 'They were the blind leading the blind' (Matthew 15:14). Enraged the Jewish leaders arranged for him to be crucified and ignored the idea of resurrection and believing he was the son of God. They denounced Christ as a magician and said 'he is in hell boiling in his own faeces' and Mary was not a virgin claiming immaculate conception but a prostitute.

The Talmud also goes on to say that the 'gentiles', anyone else but a Jew, have impure spirits and are called pigs (Jalkut Rubeni Gadol 12b) to be treated less than subhuman, the gentiles will eventually be slaves to the Jews. In essence they are against the very principle of Christian belief but it also says 'There will be false prophets'. From the conception and through the Dark Ages until today this kind of arrogant teaching and supremacy fuels war and hatred. For the religious folk of the world, this is a direct threat to their very being and belief.

Moses the prophet who declared divine connection with his god was told to go to Egypt to free the Jewish people from 400 hundred years of slavery in Egypt. After the famous exodus, the Jews roamed the desert for 40 years before Moses was ordered by his god to take them to the Promised Land where god himself would eventually live on earth with his chosen people, the Jews.

The Jews settled in their new Promised Land of Jerusalem in Israel under the divine covenant of their god, and built the first sacred temple with their King, Solomon, abiding by the rules set out in the Ten Commandments. They held the sacred 'Ark of the Covenant' along with the commandment tablets. Through debauched acts and living an unclean and immoral life, their god banished them from the land and cursed them for breaking the only divine Covenant made from God to man.

From this date the Jews have believed that they are a separate race of people, those who had the only divine contract with god. Their belief and prophecy is that they will once again be in power of their promised land, rebuild Solomon's temple and god will return and live with the Jewish people as the chosen flock. For 2,000 years they have prayed in front of the Wailing Wall hoping for forgiveness and planning for the day when Jerusalem will once again be home to the Jews, when an exact replica of Solomon's Temple will once again be built. From this time until now the Jews have been persecuted for this act of treason and betrayal of their one true god and the murder of Christ.

There are two Talmuds, one made by the Israelite Jews and the other by the Babylonians. It is believed that the Babylonian texts are more controversial with darker occult meanings and implications. The orthodox Jews are content with their religious life style and I feel no threat from their presence. But the group of Jews which are labelled 'The Zionist Jews', normally the wealthier contributors of the cult, hold a different story. The orthodox Jews are against the forced occupation of Israel, true Jews are against any violence, they oppose what the Zionist consortium are doing and yet they are labelled through their religion with the actions of a few. Religion surely should be a peaceful, self-adopting system of faith and living.

In 1666 a man called Sabbatai Sevi, a Kabalist, known as 'The Secret Lion' who declared himself the new Jewish Prophet arose in the Jewish community. His new approach to the religion was that the Torah was correct but all moral teachings should be reversed. 'Thou shalt not kill became thou shalt kill, thou shalt not commit debauched acts became thou shalt, and so on. He decreed that everything that was holy was unholy. His philosophy was that if all sin was depleted by practising daily, it would hasten the return of the Messiah. Unbelievably half of the Jewish faith joined the new cult in its new sinful form of redemption, with the belief he was the new prophet. Wife swapping and debauched acts along with orgies were practised with the motto 'redemption through sin'. Sabbatai Sevi's prayer was: 'blessed are they who permit the forbidden'.

Following his death in 1676 a new man named Jacob Frank declared to the world he was the reincarnation of Sabbatai Sevi and took on his role continuing the same belief of redemption through sin, but took it to a whole new level of satanic worship and practises.

From this period on the orthodox Jews rejected these new teachings and returned to their original canon ostracising those who wished to continue the bizarre faith.

It is believed that this satanic order continued the cult and eventually merged with Adam Weishaupt the founder of the Illuminati. This was the start of the satanic Zionist movement known as 'The Frankists' where the world's problems commenced (Ref.Sec.1).

After the eviction from most countries in the world over the years the Zionist Jews made a new stand during the birth of America in the late 1700s where they thrive today aiding the new world agenda and forcing the occupation of the 'Holy of Holies', the promised land under the guise of prophecy.

In 1917 the 'Balfour Declaration' was agreed by the Zionist Lord Rothschild and the British Crown allowing the Jewish people to return once again and own their promised land, although it was not Britain's land in the first place to be handed over, the contract was formed in exchange for help of the American armies in the First World War, aiding Britain.

Religion is not the pursuit of an educated enlightened man of true history; instead the understanding of the true meaning and circle of life gives him spiritual comfort. The corruption of religion and greed are always the two evils in life.

THE KNIGHTS TEMPLAR 1118 AD

The Knights Templar emerged in history in 1118 AD being a band of Christian monks and knights brought together for the purpose of protecting the pilgrims on the way to the Holy Land in Israel. The King of France funded a crusade to Israel with the purpose of taking control of the mount, the Holy of Holies. The Knights were to live in the temple grounds excavating the tunnels and foundations to search for the Ark of the Covenant and secret knowledge whilst protecting pilgrims from Arab attacks. The Knights succeeded in taking control of the temple ruins in Jerusalem and resided there. After some years a hidden tunnel was found containing a wooden box overlaid in solid gold with secret documents believed to hold the biggest secret of mankind, the knowledge of our true origin, the biggest scandal of all time. These artefacts were believed to have been hidden in the time of King Solomon. After hearing the news, the Count Hugh of Champagne, France the main contributor, joined the Knights to see what had been discovered. After seeing for himself he immediately gave all his wealth over to the knights crusade and became a participating knight himself. The secrets of the find were kept within the Templars Order but following the news many patrons and wealthy landowners contributed great wealth to the Knights campaign.

The Grand Master of the Templars visited Pope St Bernard and he officially ordained the Knights for their discovery which gave the Templars validation amongst the people. The Knights were also gaining a reputation for being the finest swordsmen in battle. This started a swarm of new followers who took the vow of chastity and poverty handing over their worldly goods, part of the initiation which started to make the Templars wealthy and powerful. The Order itself was to make no profit and use all money for the quest as they were under oath, with the belief that when they died they were guaranteed a place with the Lord in heaven and this is where the corruption begins! The greater your donation the better chance you would have on the Day of Judgement so the church begins to 'sell' places in heaven. As a large group of people were starting to flock to Israel to join the crusade the Templars opened the first international banking system where people could deposit money in different countries and with a receipt of payment collect their monies in Israel so as not to be mugged on route. Although no interest was charged, a handling fee was imposed. With the Templar gaining property and wealth through donation, this generated income from land tax and rents, finally leading to international money lending for the first time on a big scale.

Over a short period of time the Christian population grew in Israel, castles and small fortresses where built as they were a Christian invasion on disputed holy ground in a mostly Muslim community which I am sure did not fare well.

After nine years the Knights returned to France after completing the crusade. At this time their popularity was strong with their numbers growing steadily and their money business even stronger. Their direction changed after the realisation of how much revenue the 'religion business' was generating. They started to concentrate on lending money to royalty and kings and soon become wealthier than the kings themselves.

Philip the Fair, the King of France at this time, resented their popularity and was concerned about this new organisation overpowering his rule. So he began a religious campaign of slander against the Knights trying to bring them down accusing them of being blasphemous devil worshippers, and indulging in sexual perverse acts in their initiation ceremonies and spitting on the cross. So really no change there, history just repeats. Philip had them arrested and started to torture them in true medieval fashion forcing confessions of their alleged crimes. The Grand Master Knight was publicly burnt at the stake in 1307 AD, on Friday 13, after confessing to dishonouring the church and ungodly acts under torture. This is where for the superstitious amongst us, the unlucky Friday the 13th comes from.

The King swiftly took possession of their estates and money in a dawn raid on all known Knights Templar. Their bank in France was ceased and all assets confiscated. Although the dawn raid was successful there were many knights who fled persecution.

This ended the era of the Knights for now and after a few decades the story had faded and The Knights Templar were no more. The Catholic Church disbanded the whole organization in 1314 with all their assets confiscated. The leading Grand Masters 'The Order of the knights Templar' reformed and went underground with hatred for the Catholic Church for their betrayal and still carry the grudge today. Some believe a vast amount of money and gold that had been collected over the years left France with the escaping Templars. All these events were well documented at the time although where the treasure was taken to, no one knows for sure.

In 1187 AD the Christians lost the holy mount although they had already found what they were looking for. This piece of land is the most disputed and sacred on earth in the eyes of religion. It is the place where the most powerful king on earth in his time King Solomon lived, who held the secret Knowledge and the Ark of the Covenant. It is where the Christians and Jewish Jesus was alleged to have died and been resurrected and it is where the Anunnaki were based when they genetically created us, the only true account of gods living on this earth. Each different belief system believes in the same person, a god/creator, just with a different name. But for 3,000 years this land has been fought over time and time again causing mayhem and bloodshed for the purpose of being the owner of the only alleged divine sacred piece of land on earth, ready for the return of their god. The Jews believe it is their divine right to have the land and rebuild the temple for his return. I have always thought a sign or an email of clarification from God may be apt at this point to save the slaughter of so many innocent lives.

The Knights reformed in Scotland away from France and at the time Scotland was still fighting England over independence. The Knights were renowned for their fighting abilities and the King of Scotland enrolled them as a useful band of warriors. This is the time of the famed Robert the Bruce in the great battle against England.

Roslyn Chapel

In Scotland still today there is a church called 'The Chapel of St Matthew' in Roslyn Village. It is where the Knights Templar reformed and made an elegant structure in the same architectural layout as Solomon's Temple. Using their geometry skills and a band of stonemasons they created a spectacle of carvings throughout the church with hidden clues and esoteric meanings portraying their own crusades and suggestions of where the fabled gold and secret knowledge of our forefathers is buried. A few of the Master Templars were buried there; it was built as a shrine to their crusades and achievements. The reason the Catholic Church condemned the knights was because the knowledge that was found would have totally destroyed the whole ethos of the religious rule of the people. There is no doubt at all that the truth is known by the church, but why and how would they give up their lands and wealth and the dominating power over the masses, which they have so cleverly enforced through fear of hell and being void of an afterlife. In the Dark Ages any person not conforming to rule of the Catholic Church would be tortured and publicly burnt at the stake. They took no prisoners, any opposition suggesting the truth or a more scientific logical approach to our world came to a very abrupt end.

The Freemasons

Handed down from before the Flood to Solomon through to the Knights Templar, the secret knowledge stayed in the hands of the initiated few. The Masonic Freemasons Lodge was not officially opened as a cult until 1717 AD but the original stonemasons built wondrous churches and cathedrals including Notre-Dame 1163 AD. Architecture totally changed in these times, a new era of geometric forms were built which still stand today. The Stonemason Guild first started out as a way of keeping their building techniques secret. On meeting each other different handshakes where designed to determine instantly at what level of craftsman they were without speaking or alerting surrounding people. Placing your thumb between the finger knuckles of your fellow craftsman whilst in hand shake was a subtle acknowledgement which would go unnoticed to the uninitiated. With various different finger positions on handshakes to decipher your level or degree, the handshake was born.

In 1603 Queen Elizabeth I the Queen of England died leaving no heir to the throne so King James VI of Scotland through his birth right became King of England bringing the two lands together. At this point the Masonic fraternity on their own personal crusade took their chance to become part of England's government and elite.

Make no mistake your fellow Mason who lives in your street is not running the world or involved with blood sacrifices as the media would like you to believe. The English Masonic brethren are actually very charitable people and regularly have meetings involving raising money for good causes. As all cults and belief groups there is a hierarchical system in place where different levels of initiation are implemented and those in lower degrees would be unaware of the full implications of what they have joined. The American French and English Masons all have their own dealings and work rosters, the agenda of American Masons cannot be linked to the English system or morals. The media have misinformed us for centuries and because it is a secret society, people have made many assumptions about and accusations of, the cult.

In 1717 the Freemasons opened the first official Grand Lodge in Queens Street, London, coming together at the Goose and Gridiron Tavern in St Paul's churchyard, with Anthony Sayer being elected the Grand Master.

Apart from being a cult with its own belief system based on secret knowledge going back to King Solomon, it is an unbiased group of businessmen who frequently meet and exchange ideas. Being a member of this group opens doors which otherwise would not be available, due to the diversity of people involved, from royalty to layman. Whether the leaders of the world are party to the Masonic Order has no relevance, it just indicates, depending on their degree, initiation into a secret society of world truth and secrecy. From the Masons many other groups have formed like 'The Skull and Cross Bones' in America, a very controversial group with bizarre rituals made up of world leaders and corporate fat cats. Again, some of these will be Masonic but the individual person or corporations running the world today are not flying the flag of either group it is just a way of meeting and coming together with the same beliefs and practising rituals handed down the centuries.

THE ROMAN CATHOLIC CHURCH

The Vatican City in Rome, Italy is the remnant of the mighty Roman Empire. It is classed as an independent 'Sovereign State' since 1929 controlled under its own rules, with its own currency and bank, so is tax exempt. It is spread over 100 acres and has a population of 826 people, enclosed by a fortress wall. The church through selling positions in heaven and confiscating lands from the Inquisition days in the Middle Ages collected an empire world wide of wealth and property producing incomes for centuries off the back of their misdeeds.

In 1252 AD the Inquisition was established and authorised the use of torture by Pope Innocent IIII, quite ironically, to root out suspected heresy, people who did not hold the faith and gospel of the Roman church. The church at this point held power throughout Europe over the people and ruled with an iron sword over kings and nobles. Those who did not practise the doctrine or who were suspected of worshipping other faiths or in fact any kind of forward thinking in the arts and sciences were arrested and held. All worldly goods were taken then tortured to confess their alleged sins, then killed in many painful forms. All past history of our true origin was completely eradicated from all written sources and deemed heresy even if the subject was spoken of. Education did not exist in those days illiteracy was common, it was only the church, monks and royalty who had funds to educate themselves.

In 1487 a book was published by Pope Innocent VIII for the purpose of clarifying the description of who was and who was not a witch. Any one practising the art of herbal healing instead of the will of god, or visionaries, tarot readers or science of any kind would be deemed a heretic accused of having a pact with the devil and would be burnt at the stake. Thousands of women suffered this persecution and some as young as nine were sent to the torture towers. It is no wonder the art of alchemy and forward thinking scholars of the time formed secret groups to keep their practises hidden on fear of death or incarceration. This is the era due to the barbaric rule of the Catholic Church where many brotherhoods were formed.

Pope Innocent III declared that anyone who attempts to control a personal view of god which conflicts with church dogmas must be burnt at the stake without pity. From 1229 onwards an estimated one million people came to a bloody and torturous end by the Inquisition all in the name of rule and their all loving god. Most of the splendour and majesty seen today in the Vatican and the Sistine Chapel is money collected from the persecution of innocent people and confiscation in the renaissance when their corruption was at its ugliest.

You would expect that such a significant event as the crucifixion and resurrection of Christ would have numerous accounts by the writers of that time. There was

Flavius Josephus the Jewish scribe, and Tacitus and Suetonius the Roman historians who wrote accepted true contemporary historical accounts of their time. All of these historians wrote very little, amounting to a few sentences at best, relating only to a subject called 'Christ' which only means 'The anointed one'. Matthew, Mark, Luke and John, the original scribes, which strangely are English names not Hebrew, wrote the story approximately 150 years later with contradictory accounts, as none of them were there at the event. The resurrection of Christ after the crucifixion and the virginal purity of his mother Mary is the pinnacle of the faith of Christianity and the Catholic Church, without this there is no religion.

I have never studied another religion's history in which it preaches love and redemption that has persecuted and cruelly murdered and tortured men women and children for such a long period of time, for the sake of protecting the story of the resurrection of a fabled man. Religion has brought war and division of mankind and unclarified false hope. Is this the will of their God?

My understanding of this religion is that there is one god who created the entire universe. He gave us rules to live by and sent his son to die for us. If we worship and adore him and abide by his rules and follow the teachings of Jesus, we will live for eternity in heaven with the one god. But if we go against these rules we are sent to hell and burn for eternity in fire and brimstone. But, he loves us.

The Bible tells us that the universe and the beginning of all things were created in 4,404 BC by their one god, with strangely no mention of the 177 million years of dinosaurs. He made Adam, the first man, and after Lilith, Adams first wife. The Bible tells us Lilith was disobedient to Adam so god made another called Eve. Adam and Eve started the population as we know today although their sons married, to whom did they marry?

After just 2,000 years he looked upon the earth and saw that 'the wickedness of man was great on the earth and it was corrupt'. He decreed to punish the wicked and disobedient "I will destroy man whom I have created from the face of the earth: both man, beast and the creeping thing and the fouls of the air: for it repenteth me that I have made them" (Genesis 6:7) He sent a great flood to Earth to destroy and wipe out all men, women, children and beast, good or bad allowing only Noah's family and the chosen animals to re-start the population once more. This act seems far from just or fair for the innocent people of the world, not the work of a loving caring god.

The misconception and the biggest lie to mankind is that there is not one all knowing all seeing god, the creation of man, according to historic finds, belongs to a superior race of beings, a group of people, perceived to be gods, by early man who once visited earth.

The earth alone is 450 billion years old, the universe has no known age. To believe the conception of the universe and all things happened 6000 years ago is fantasy and can only be humoured.

On the opposite side, religion has been engraved and enforced into our society for centuries and has brought comfort for many who need a crutch and an alternative to the possible reality of death and non-existence at the end of their life. The basic aspect of religion is a comforting faith for many but the reality, as all major corporations; it is corrupt and fuelled by deceit, power and greed. The church's wealth could comfortably feed the millions of starving people of this world but it chooses not to.

As the religious faith becomes transparent and the churches are being sold off in England, the Catholic Church is bringing the world's religions together to form a 'one world religion' to save the faith and its empire. For the church to continue as a faith of hope, it must be revised and accept the scientific facts of our past and stop living in denial, take a fresh approach of spiritual afterlife.

The Christian and Catholic religion is a parody on the worship of the sun. It is Pagan based with astrological symbolic symbols throughout the Vatican if only the flock were to look. Many of the Bible stories are plagiarised copies of ancient Egyptian and Sumerian history well before Christ ever existed, it is simply a system of rule and suppression over the masses. Blind faith is a perfect concept as you never see it. It preys on the weak and vulnerable and willingly accepts payment for their practise.

Pope Leo X famously said "What profit has not that fable of Christ?"

Man made god, god didn't make man.

AMERICA

The first proven people to discover the continent of America, contrary to belief, were the Vikings in Newfoundland in 1,000 AD followed by the Chinese in around 1420 AD in the area of California. Our history books tell us that Columbus (Cristoforo Colombo) the Italian explorer first discovered America in 1492 but in fact he was the person who started the colonisation of the country, it is always the victors who write the bias history.

Columbus came to America with nothing but a few ships, no land and no claim to any of the country. Interestingly the flags which flew on his ships were a red cross on a white background; this was the symbol of the Knights Templar.

In 1776 on 4 July the 'Declaration of Independence' from England was established following the revolutionary war. A law system was soon introduced in 1787 to produce tax from the people to pay for the debt of the war and continue stealing land from the Indians and create their own country. Black slavery was soon exploited using free labour to monopolise on the cotton and sugar beet fields which fuelled immigration and attracted capitalists.

Land-greedy and ambitious people flocked from all round the world including Europe to stake a claim on land that already belonged to the indigenous Indians, people who had lived in peace for thousands of years. The religious invaders believed it was the will of god that these lands should be theirs and they proceeded to occupy from the Atlantic to the pacific displacing and colonising any land and indigenous people in their wake.

In 1830 President Andrew Jackson signed the 'Indian Removal Act' which instigated the forced removal of all Indian tribes from the east. On an 800 mile forced trek by foot at gunpoint, all Indians where forced west and made to evacuate their homeland, many were killed and others died of exhaustion.

This first act of many went down in the Indian's history as 'The Trail of Tears' for its brutal and inhumane forced exodus of good people from their own land.

What a beautiful country it would have been if it had been left alone for the Indians to live in peace and harmony with nature as man was born to be.

Through ignorance of litigation in contract and the fact they did not speak our language, more than 500 treaties were made and broken under the new law of the land, not their law, the law of the invaders. They already owned the land; they had no written law or wanted one. The new Americans advanced from east to west stealing their land, murdering men, women and children displacing the tribes and pushing them into ever smaller areas. Ethnic cleansing it was called.

The economic growth was based around exploiting slave labour in the 1800 and 1900s exporting low cost crops among many other slave labour based commodities like mining minerals which needed minimal labour costs.

In 1823 the US Supreme Court/Johnson and Grahams Lessee V McIntosh ruled that the first nations of occupancy 'The United States of America' has unequivocally agreed that discovery gave an exclusive right to extinguish the Indian title of occupancy.

The Indian Appropriations Act of 1871 legislation ruled that it ceases to recognise Indian nationals as sovereign which gave the right to seize all of their lands breaking all previous treaties.

"It is my purpose to utterly exterminate the Sioux; they are to be treated as maniacs or wild beasts and by no means as people with whom treaties or compromise can be made." General John Pope US army.

From 1871-1910 the government laid siege to the buffalo which was the main source of livelihood for the Indians providing clothes, tepees food and trade. The government began aiding the slaughter giving free ammunition and supplies to anyone wishing to help the quest. In 1873 alone it is recorded that 1.5 million buffalo where pointlessly slaughtered. Later in some regions money was paid for the scalps of Indians fuelling legal murder.

"Having wronged the Indians for centuries we had better, in order to protect our civilisation, follow it up by one more wrong and wipe these untamed and untameable creatures from the face of the earth". Frank Baum editorial in the Aberdeen Saturday Pioneer 1891.

General George Custer in the US army in 1874 publicly announced that he had found gold in the 'Black Hills' in South Dakota, the burial grounds of the ancient Indian chiefs. In 1875 the US demanded that the Indians sell the gold ridden hills even though they had pledged to protect the sacred burial grounds of their ancestors through treaties made by the American government.

This episode of breaking the treaties on sacred land led to 'The Battle of Little Big Horn' in the 'Great Sioux War' of 1876-1877 between the Indians and the United States. George Custer was killed but alas the land was still taken.

By 1889 the US government started to sell the land of the Sioux Indians. They divided it in to sections and sold to the highest bidder with expectations of finding gold. They were determined to eliminate the whole life and history of these people.

In 1890 on 29 December the government sent the 7th Cavalry with 500 troops armed with rapid fire Gatling guns to surround 'Big Foots' Sioux Indians who were armed with bow and arrows at 'Loudy Creek'. On this day they slaughtered 312 innocent men women and children.

Twenty-three US troops were given the Medal of honour for this genocide at the battle that went down in history as 'The Battle of Wounded Knee'.

"Something else died here in the bloody mud and was buried in the blizzard. A people's dream died here. It was a beautiful dream, the nation's hope is broken and scattered. There is no centre any longer and the secret tree is dead." Black Elk (the Warrior and medicine man of the Oglala Lakota Indians).

This is the story of the indigenous Indian tribes of America like the Sioux, Apache, Cheyenne and Blackfoot in America that were brutally murdered and suppressed. From the 1700s to the present day these peace loving people have been fighting for a small piece of land to call their own so they can continue their way of life, the land which was rightly theirs in the beginning.

THE ROTHSCHILDS

Although the world is made up of 195 independent Sovereign States which are run by their own governments, there is one family which controls most of the flow of money throughout the world to each individual country, the Rothschilds Bank. In 1743 in the town of Frankfurt in Germany a counting house, a bullion agent, was trading under the name of Amschel Moses Bower. Above the door hung their sign or coat of arms which was a Roman eagle on a red background and the company was known as the 'Red Shield' firm. When Amschel Mayer Bower, his son, inherited the business in the early 1800s he decided to change his family name to 'Rothschild' which in German means 'red shield'. They soon learnt that lending money to the nobles and governments of the world was much more lucrative than to the individual persons and the payments were secured from the nation's tax payers. The debt of a country, normally down to mismanagement, is loaned on the security of the people themselves.

The father sent five of his sons, Amschel, Carl, Salomon, Nathan and Jacob to different countries to set up office and expand their loaning empire. Amschel stayed in Frankfurt to take care of the central office, Carl was sent to Naples, Salomon was based in Vienna, Jacob to Paris and the brightest Nathan aged 21 was sent to London England.

It is important to understand how the Rothschilds managed to be in the position to loan vast amounts of money to the kings and nobles to fully understand their position today. In 1815 the great battle of Waterloo was fought on Belgian soil with Napoleon Bonaparte leading the French Empire into battle against the British army, commanded by The Duke of Wellington supported by the seventh coalition and Prussian army commanded by Gebhard Von Blucher. Both sides of the war needed funding and the rule of Europe was at stake. So the Rothschilds being neutral having banks in both countries, loaned the money to both sides. War was and still is the most profitable business in the world for war profiteers like the Bankers and suppliers of weapons.

In 1814 Prince William IX of Hesse-Hanau had entrusted to Mayer Amschel Rothschild the sum of $3 million for safe keeping and in these days this was a fortune. Instead Mayer invested his money in gold to fund and profit from the Napoleons war. Nathan stationed an agent called Rothworth near the border of France with plans of getting the news of the victor of the battle before anyone else. He received the news 24 hours before it hit the stock exchange and so was in a lead position. By manipulating the English stock exchange he started to sell all his stocks which caused a panic amongst the other traders thinking that Napoleon must have won the war. So all stocks over night sank to an all time low. Nathan then using outside agents bought back the stocks at a fraction of the cost succeeding in becoming wealthier than the Bank of England itself over night.

By the mid-18th century the Rothschild family was purported to be the wealthiest establishment in the world. They proceeded to finance the building of the railways and diamond mining in Africa and any other venture like the British steel industry that needed funding. Loaning money and mingling with such people as dukes and royalty. Being court bankers, of course brings power and influence over the running of society itself. You have the power to sanction or in fact stop the flow of money to any party you choose. If a country is performing acts that are contrary to your investment and you are the supplier of their finance, then you have full power and influence to change decisions. Be under no illusion this breed of person has no consideration or compassion what so ever for the common man. Sending young men to die in wars that they don't understand, and are too young to comprehend, just to earn more money for their greed and insanity is common practice, they have no soul.

Amschel Rothschild famously said "I care not who controls a nation's political affairs so long as I control her currency" and Nathan Rothschild said "The man who controls Britain's money supply controls the British Empire and I control the British money supply".

CHAPTER 3

UNDERSTANDING ENGLAND'S PERSPECTIVE

Two thousand years ago native Britain was separate from Scotland and Wales and was made up of small settlements which was ruled by the wealthy and held together by Pagan belief and monasteries. Unique to the rest of Europe we were an island which gave us the advantage over mainland invasions of conquering powers. In 43 AD the Roman Empire who had taken control of Europe, North Africa and was working east, descended on Britain with 40,000 solders with the quest to conquer, rule and exploit financially the rich lands and enslave the people. The British lacked the sophisticated training of the Roman soldiers and although we fought for several years, Emperor Claudius finally took over the rule of Britain giving the island the name of Britannia.

For 400 years the Romans held their position although not always peacefully with civil wars breaking out against the rule with People like 'Boadicea' or Boudica the famous Welsh female warrior who led the Brits against the Romans. Although we were a suppressed enslaved nation under rule, this era bought the first roads networks, stone architecture, new foreign crops, European trade and a structured society which would fare well in our future.

In 367 AD the British island attracted new enemies, new powers wanting to pillage our lands. The Germans came along, the Germanic Saxons approaching from the north and east raiding the coastal towns which put strain on the roman occupancy.

Following continuous invasions in the Roman heartland itself the Romans pulled out in 408 AD to stabilise the empire leaving Britannia to fend for itself, but we regained freedom.

Britannia itself did not start its own world Empire until late in history once we had mastered the art of producing warships and defending our coast line in the 1600s. As the Roman army had left, this made the island vulnerable to whoever considered themselves mighty enough to take the island by force. With the Romans interbreeding for 400 years, the Vikings from Denmark in 878 AD and the French at the end of the decade the true blood line of England was already quite diverse.

In 1066 AD Britain stabilised into what is considered the start of the royal blood lines which are present today. On 14 October William the Duke of Normandy, France defeated Harold II of England at the Battle of Hastings. On Christmas Day of that year he was crowned the first French King of England. At this time the crown was not inherited it was elected by the bishops and leading nobility. William went on to divide the lands of the country into shires and gave his knights and bishops who helped conquer Britain their own sections of land. They swore allegiance to the new King and governed their new shires with the duty of collecting taxes for William known as the feudal system, taxpaying tenants of the King. The church system still holding their ground on the rule of society had no choice but to agree and compromise with the new French ruling king but William allowed the cult to continue under his supervision. William the conqueror is believed to be responsible for the construction of the Tower of London where he lived in 1078.

THE DOOMSDAY BOOK 1086 AD

King William the conqueror was responsible for the 'Doomsday Book' aptly named by the people which was the first account in England where every piece of land and person was registered and logged along with livestock and machinery so that the King could maximise the amount of tax he could pilfer from every person and landowner in Britannia, so the aristocracy rule and taxation of the people started.

HENRY VIII 1491-1547

THE START OF THE BRITANNIA EMPIRE

Henry VIII was the king who turned Britannia around, the man who stopped outside invasion and armed the island with the finest fleet of warships equipped with the first cast iron cannons, the most famous being the 'The Marie Rose', although sadly due to incompetent crew, she sank close to English shores fully laden. The French and Spanish galleons where always a threat to the English fleet but after the Battle of Trafalgar where the Spanish and Portuguese were obliterated England had established a defensive naval fleet unbeatable by the world.

We went on to conquer the world from the shores of Australia down to the Caribbean, India, South Africa Canada and America, by the early 1900s Britain ruled half of the world, Colonial rule, 'ordered progress' we called it. Taking over other parts of the world, stealing their minerals and wealth replacing it with a civilised system ruled by ourselves. The Spanish and Portuguese went on to conquer South America and so the world was divided up into different sovereign states much like they are today.

It was not until 1688 that the people of England had any rights in society. The great Revolution of England known as 'The Glorious Revolution' of 1688 was the uprising of the English people overthrowing King James II who wished Roman Catholicism to be reinstated. By a union of Parliamentarians, they banned any Catholics from inheriting the throne finally ending the brutal influence of the Roman Catholic Church. The Dutch stadtholder, William III, Prince of Orange, married Mary II and they become king and queen of England.

The new system of invasion of other countries today is subtle and less brutal than the old times although the end product is still the same. We would have hoped that mass murder of innocent people in other countries for material gain would have ceased after two world wars and various other massacres over the last century but it continues.

There are advantages of being an island now that we have voted to shed the shackles and grip of the European Union law. This country needs a true leader, a person with a backbone not a tail, someone who will lead and serve the people for the country's good, not sell his soul for his own gain. England once had a fine flourishing fishing industry which gave the people of the coast prospects, futures and a way of earning money to feed their families.

In 1983 the EU served England a fishing quota and fishing limits for our own seas, where and how much we were allowed to catch. Overnight the whole of England's coastal fishing industries shut down after 2,000 years of a thriving business, reduced to 10 percent of its former glory, one of England's staple diets for centuries. Since then we have imported our own fish from our own seas caught by the Europeans.

Also in 1983 the Conservatives mutilated the coal industry and shut down most of the coal mines in Britain sending 193,000 people to the dole queue and rendering whole towns desolate and poverty stricken. Later the iron industry that led the world was also attacked and reduced to a sorry state again leaving thousands out of work and whole towns being redundant. We once produced vast amounts of our own produce for our own use and enough for export, building the economy giving us local quality food, not using GMO or other carcinogenic pesticides which riddle us with diseases which we import today. We were once self-sufficient with enough jobs and industries that had served us well for hundreds of years. We can do this again given the correct leader allowing our country to be independently run again rather than being suppressed and influenced by the world leaders, power and greed. Do what you will but leave the common man alone, do not incarcerate our lifestyle any more than you already have. Let us live free and healthy with human rights and the chance to leave a legacy to our down line that we can be proud of.

English politics took a downward spiral and changed for ever when in 1979 the leader of the Conservative party Margaret Thatcher took office to lead the people of Great Britain. Margaret Thatcher was a complete disgrace to the working class people of England, she fought against the very people who voted her in to power. She divided the people and tried to break the unions, the only protective legislation that the workers have for fair working conditions. She brought chaos, hatred and poverty to the streets causing division between the working class. As a true Conservative she privatised many of the nation's businesses, England was up for sale. The Conservatives whilst in power helped destroy England's three main industries, metal, fish and coal. It crippled England and scared the people; England has not fully recovered since.

If you need a job to live and you have nothing to conserve, then never vote for Conservative rule. These people never have and never will have any interest or support for the working class people of England. We are a number, nothing more nothing less that generates tax for the crown in the eyes of the Conservatives. A commodity that they squeeze and suppress at every given opportunity. The conservatives represent and serve the interests of the capitalists and corporates of England.

London's inner square mile is a privately owned City State, a corporation located right in the centre of greater London which dates back to the Roman invasion, symbolised by the Egyptian obelisk called Cleopatra's Needle representing the pagan sun god of ancient Egypt Ra. It became a Sovereign State in 1694 when King William III privatised the Bank of England. Today it is the world's financial trading centre housing the Rothschild controlled Bank of England, Lloyds of London, the London Stock Exchange, and many other foreign banks. It has its own 'The Right Honourable Lord Mayor of London' separate from the City's Mayor, and its own courts, laws and police force and is named 'The City Corporation of London'. The Lord Mayor and 12 Council Members serve as representatives for the world's wealthiest most powerful banking families which are situated in the City, including the Rothschilds, the Warburg family, the Oppenheimer family and the Schiff family. These families and associates, through the generations have held power and trade within the City Corporation of London.

THE BIRTH OF INCARCERATION

We the people think we are free but this is just an illusion created by the system we were born into with no choice of our own. On our birth certificate we were given a number which indicates we are the property of this country. We must abide by the rules of the land and pay taxes to the crown. At the age of four we are sent to school by law to be programmed by a regimental system preparing us for a life of work for 50 years with which the system gives us no choice, a life of paying tax to the ruling class. The schooling system crushes any free thinking we may have and places us in a tight box filling us with untrue history and a biased explanation of the world we live in. Consider the world as a fabricated system of incarceration, we being the workforce and owned by a landlord. We are a commodity in the eyes of the Crown that generates taxes herded like sheep and controlled by rule. No one owns us as individual people, it is our right to live free.

In the beginning we were content growing are own crops and trading amongst ourselves. The ruling class after the Doomsday Book started to impose taxes on all people in England with or without land because they could and had the enforcement to impose it. Slavery, mainly African at the time, was a free commodity as people were forcibly enslaved and sold on as a working animal, a commodity, and was treated as such.

The disadvantage of owning a slave is that they have to be housed and fed and this becomes costly and inefficient. So they created a system where the human animal believes they are free and let them pay for their own house and living and just take half of what they earn, free range slaves. Create a religion as moral fibre and further suppression for a special place to go when you die if you obey the rules, and create a hell for those who do not. Suppressing the masses is nothing new, it has been happening for centuries but now in this era with worldwide public media owned by the very corporations that rule us, we are entering an extremely dangerous period which we all need to be aware of and the direct implications to you.

Today we think we have the freedom to nominate a member of our society by the people for the people to govern our land fairly in the best interest of our liberty. Always they rule us, not serve us, it is a completely staged fabrication of lies and dogmatics. Everyone has their price and many leaders sell their soul for their own gain.

The independent corporate companies like the oil barons, the drug suppliers, the seed cartel and the food producers of each country have a large proportion of the flow of monies generated by the masses but they are owned by the people who fund them, the world Bankers.

Without freedom for the people it will kill diversity, without diversity there is no life. One world governing dictatorship unrivalled, will destroy man.

George Orwell wrote "The ruling class in every age have tried to impose a false view of the world upon their followers" (AM Heath 2003 'Animal Farm and 1984'. p289)

CHAPTER 4

THE BLUEPRINT CONNECTION

Now please pay attention and read carefully, this is where today's worlds predicament started and how our situation is escalating into a non-reversible state of decline and suppressed human freedom. Where one governing body rules from the dark corners of world politics wishing to control all banking, abolish human rights, control all food supplies and take away our basic human freedom using a biased dictatorship.

In 1776 a Jesuit priest named John Adam Weishaupt founded a new cult called the 'Illuminati' in Bavaria. He was a doctor of law and a professor by the age of 24, an educated man, armed with the rudiments and the passion of a lunatic. His aim was to recruit people from the elite and world ruling bodies who would join him in his quest for financially ruling and incarcerating the human population of the world.

In 1717 the Freemason fraternity was established and Weishaupt approached the order as a top potential recruiting ground for new members of his cult. By 1790 it is estimated that they were 2,000 strong reaching most countries across Europe. In 1773 Bavaria declared a ban on all secret societies, Weishaupt fled the country and so the cult went underground. 'The Owl of Minerva' was the original symbol of the Illuminati, not the all-seeing eye as many think. The very same owl is used and worshipped at the Bilderberg's meetings once a year.

AMERICA GAINED INDEPENDENCE IN 1776

Following the defeat of the English at the Battle of York Town, top world financiers found their chance to own and govern a huge new land mass on the other side of the world. After independence had been won and the financial support and governing system of Britain had been taken away, the new Americans had difficulty in funding any growth or in fact making a system of law with a country so large.

A group of elites from round the world, capital investors, bankers and political adversaries started the American Law as we know it today. Later a company called 'The Corporation of the United States' was formed giving the rule of the country to a business group, a corporation, a private business outside of the original American constitution. This group of signatories were 56 strong with 50 being Freemasons.

SKULL AND CROSS BONES 1833

The 'Skull and Cross Bones' is an American cult which is rarely mentioned in the public domain due to its political members. It was formed in 1833 as another more exclusive secret society. The sign of the 'Skull and Bones' is of course taken from the era of the pirates 150 years previous or perhaps just continued. The motto of the pirates, the Captain Morgan's and the Black Beards of the Caribbean was 'Take all you can and give nothing back'. Well nothing seems to have changed there then! If you start to study the genetic family lines of the people who have been in power in the United States of America and England you will soon discover that the table is bent and the whole voting system is a complete fabrication, it is the same clan with a different figurehead, these family ties go back centuries.

1908 CRUDE OIL WAS DISCOVERED IN IRAN

In 1908 Great Britain decided that oil was to be the future of the world replacing coal and set up a company called the 'Anglo Persian Oil Company' to develop newly discovered oil fields in Iran. Huge investments were made by the British government and other wealthy investors on land at that time, ruled by the Ottoman/Turkish regime.

1914 FIRST WORLD WAR

Germany decided to expand its borders and declared war on Russia on 1 August 1914. The Ottomans sided with Germany/Austria and Hungary which put the English in a tight spot. Their huge oil investment was at great risk.

In November 1914 England under the command of 'The First Lord of Admiralty' Winston Churchill, sent troops to Basra in Iran to defend the oil fields and their investment company. In March 1917 the British took Bagdad by force ending with 9,000 Turkish people surrendering instead of death by war. The British went on to capture the town of

Mosul which meant they had most of the control of Iraq, the Ottoman Turks where defeated. At the 'Peace Conference' in Paris 1919 at the League of Nations it was declared that France and Britain would divide the lands and rule the region.

A major event transpired here when Iraq and Palestine became a mandate entrusted to Britain. Britain declared to the people that they would help rebuild their integral political and social systems but on the condition that they ruled and held the power over the people and would dictate which person would hold office. In 1920 Iraq revolted against the British but after three months of war the British remained in power.

1917 OCTOBER

THE BALFOUR DECLARATION

The Balfour Declaration was an agreement between America and England stating that America would send troops to aid in the First World War and help England, promising to give them Palestine. Palestine at this time was not owned by Britain but the deal was done. America agreed and joined forces with England against Germany and the war was won.

WAR PROFITEERS

American corporate giants such as Henry Ford supplied both sides of the war. The vehicles that propelled the troops in Germany and tanks that killed the American soldiers were supplied by Mr Ford. The Tetra ethanol needed to fuel their planes was supplied by the American based oil companies. Wars and the supply of war machinery is one of the biggest money generating operations, money over death.

An estimated 9 million people died in the First World War.

The way to predict the future is to make it, if you own and have the power over what the media prints and what the journalists report, you control the direction and influence over the people, if you own the money you own the world, it is a rich man's game.

1913 THE FEDERAL BANK

1913 was the year that the people of America sold their soul. Woodrow Wilson the president of America along with the congress signed the 'Federal Reserve Act' which entitled a privately owned company to control the money flow of America. The Federal Bank wrote their own rules and regulations and called it 'The Federal Reserve Act'. This act was then passed by the elected leader of the people, Woodrow Wilson, in return for financing and supporting his own election campaign.

Later Woodrow Wilson was purported to have said "I have unwittingly ruined my country; a great industrial nation is now controlled by its system of credit. We are no longer a government by free option, no longer a government of free conviction and the vote of the majority but a government by the opinion and duress of a small group of dominant men".

1914 UNDERSTANDING ISRAEL AND PALESTINE

The British moved in and occupied Palestine in 1914 ending the Muslim rule. They promised the Arab states in 1917 independence including Palestine although through the Balfour Declaration, the country had already been signed over to America for help with the First World War.

The Jews were only 8% of the population in Palestine at this time but gradually the population grew and in 1948 they established and were granted 'The State of Israel' a place for all the Jews to live once more.

Thousands of resident Palestinians were forced out of their houses over the coming 60 years as the Jewish population grew with many returning home to what they call their divine right by order of God.

Palestine fights against Israel for their forced occupation of their Land. But the American corporation supports and financially aids Israel and have many invested interests. Cutting through the bureaucracy this is the simplified situation.

Gamel Abdul Nasser, former President of United Arab Republic was purported to have said in a live interview "I cannot respect the present Jews because they left Israel black and came back white".

Forced occupation/colonisation of a country in our times today, is a direct violation of United Nations resolutions but it's allowed to continue. Who runs the UN? It has the blueprint of the American Indians which is still ongoing.

1921 HITLER THE NAZI LEADER

Adolf Hitler is one of the most misunderstood characters in past history. Adolph was born in Austria in 1889 near the German border with ambitions of becoming an artist. With an aggressive father and his mother dying young he was brought up in a catholic monastery from the age of six. After failing to be accepted twice by the academy of art in his early teens he became a traveller but with no funding he found himself in Vienna living in a hostel for homeless people.

When the First World War was declared he joined the German army and soon climbed the ranks to Corporal and was awarded the Iron Cross for his bravery whilst in the trenches on the front line.

In 1921 Hitler became leader of 'The Nationalist Party' the Nazi right wing and led the movement against the communists who were 6 million strong at the time. Protesters were often confronted at their public meetings as the German people were anti-Nazi. The communists organised a police barrier on one of their marches and shot Hitler. Hitler survived although he was arrested and later jailed for treason and sentenced to five years in prison. This only strengthened his cause in anti-communist rule and his following became stronger and after just nine months he was released from prison.

He declared to the Germans that he would stand strong and fight for the people against the Jewish Zionists who had suppressed their lives for so long. He offered the people a dream from a person who had lived through the poverty and suppression himself. He told his people that they were the chosen race. He saw the manipulation and corrupt dealings of the world leaders first hand in the First World War, he gained vital experience to lead his campaign against the world's common enemy. If you study the translations of his speeches to the nation it clearly states the reasons for persecuting the Jews. But as I mentioned before you cannot blame the entire Jewish race for the actions of the greedy few, it is often the minority who poison the water of many.

Hitler was an eccentric, no different to any other parasite who wishes to conquer and control the world and rule all people. But like all parasites, if untreated, they will eventually take control. He believed he was the descendant of the Aryan race, the blue eyed fabled race of people from the times of Atlantis. He formed a special unit called 'Vrill' which travelled the world searching for the truth of ancient history run by Heinrich Himmler, his second in command. He went as far as Antarctica looking for the inner world where a huge army base was constructed. He was obsessed with creating the perfect 'white race', eliminating any genetic defaults in the human population. He believed it was his destiny and right to rule the new master race. As a cult fanatic, to manifest his dream, all opposition would be eliminated through eugenics and racial purity with only the pure bloodline of the Aryan's saved.

Hitler massacred thousands of Jews, first using them to build underground military bases then gassing them to death, his way of eliminating the Zionist Jew problem. The primary reason for his war was to eliminate the corruption, suppression and escalating world rule of the Zionist Jews which hounded the people of his country. The fascist control of Europe today, being forced upon the European people is the same enemy that Hitler was fighting 73 years ago.

Although all of the victims of the war were not Jews, all of the Jews were victims. Putting WW2 into perspective you must understand that an estimated 56.4 million people lost their lives with 3 million being Jewish. Yet the story told of this war always holds emphasis on Hitler killing the Jews. Consider the other 53 million innocent souls who gave their lives from many different countries, why are they forgotten in the story? Eradicating the Jews was his main aim as it was the race of people who he believed to be the source of his enemy. But in fact the Jewish loss is a very small percentage of victims. The victors always write the history. All wars are unnecessary atrocities and always the innocent suffer.

A small village called 'Oradour-Sur-Glane' in Haute-Vienne, France seems to be the forgotten atrocity which happened to the French people just months before the end of the war. On 10 June 1944 the German Waffen-SS Company entered this small village in France and massacred all the inhabitants. 642 innocent men, women and children died that day. The men were rounded up and shot and the women and children were locked in the church and were burnt to death with no mercy. This village stands today untouched since the atrocity as a memorial to those who died and the persecution of innocent people under Nazi rule.

What is good for the human race is not always good for the individual person. The idea of eliminating genetic bloodlines of imperfection and creating one perfect modified race of people has its own problems. The same in nature is true, we need diversity and freedom to go forward. If everything is regimented and strictly controlled which is today's agenda, there is no space for human invention or imagination. Nature has been successfully running this planet for 450 billion years and we need to understand and accept, that by far, this should be the chosen way, it works. We have grown and bonded together as part of this unique rock of ours but we need to learn peace. Our whole genetic human form and existence is owed to planet earth, it is our home, there is no other place to go! We must start to respect and treat it as our friend instead of allowing a handful of greedy egotistical leaders to plunder the Earth's riches for their own gain and selfish needs. It is not too late to turn the tables, we could make our world a better place.

Adolf Hitler wrote a book called 'Mein Kampf' which was banned for many years explaining the truth of his actions and why he carried out the atrocities known to us all. First read the book written by Adolf Hitler himself and read the truth. What he was fighting for then, is still the war we all have today. What the world rulers have in store for our future is not a pretty picture, Hitler lost the war, and the enemy is still at large, always look at the bigger picture. It is important to note that you don't have to be a Jew to be Zionist. A Zionist is someone who wishes to develop and protect the State of Israel.

In 2015 the President of Israel, Benjamin Netanyahu made a public speech at the Third World Congress announcing the biggest lie of the past 100 years, causing controversy of course. He said that the Grand Mufti of Jerusalem, Hakuju Mini Hussain an ally of Hitler at this time, had said that, if you expel the Jews, the Jews would return to Israel. Hitler asked what is to be done with them? The Mufti replied, we do not want them, burn them instead. The truth about the Promised Land is not as perceived, the politics goes much deeper. Forced Zionist control of Palestine is the agenda, not the biblical prophecy the orthodox Jews pray for. It seems it will become a capitalist, Zionist owned country. Is it really going to be the home land for all Jews, or just the chosen flock?

After the Germans where defeated and war stopped, America stepped in and ordered all the specialist scientists and aviation experts of Hitler's army to be bought direct to America to be used in 'Operation Paper Clip', with a secret amnesty for all war crimes. Germany was leading the world in aviation and flying saucer prototypes at this time. America wanted the knowledge, the American corporation wanted to conquer the world, Germany was not going to stand in their way. America armed the war in many ways as well as the Zionist Jews, who owned German banks. (Ref. Sec 3.)

WORLD WAR TWO 1939

By 1922 following the German defeat, the country was on a downward spiral with inflation leaping skywards and property and businesses plummeting to an all time low, Germany was up for sale to the highest bidder. Huge reparation costs of World War I were served to the country with restrictions for the people and sanctions on trade which crippled its economy and bought the country to its knees, people were starving. The wealthy Jews among other top capitalists around the world took advantage of Germany's predicament and invested heavily in the city.

For the German people at this time life was not looking great, the whole of Europe publicly humiliated these people. Many Germans living in Poland were run out of their homes, murdered and persecuted. A wave of genocide soon spread throughout the west of Poland in a region called Prussia where a large population of the Germans lived.

The British Empire and America had also been severely wounded, financially drained and it was something which they were not going to take lightly, Germany was considered the aggressor amongst the Euro countries and the leading world. Before the Second World War was declared France, England and America were prepared to attack Germany if they decided to declare war on any other country in Europe.

In 1939 with the continuous assaults by the Polish on the German people of their country and with Hitler in charge, he declared war on Poland.

On 2 September 1939 England gave Germany an ultimatum 'leave the occupancy of Poland within 24 hours or England will declare war on you'.

On the 3 September 1939 England declared war on Germany which started the Second World War. England and France at this time where the biggest landowners in the world and were not going to allow Germany to infringe upon the empires. The American corporation was well underway on its own quest for world domination in the shadows of politics. They had to join the war to protect their own agenda and investments of ruling Europe by contract, starting the European Union.

MAY 10 1940

Winston Churchill became Prime Minister of the United Kingdom and led the war. Hitler quickly seized Paris which shocked the world. The French surrendered and British troops then outnumbered and out manoeuvred, were forced back to the shores of our Island in the Battle of Dunkirk. Eventually in 1939 on 1 September Germany surrendered after the alleged suicide of Hitler and the war was over in Europe. America offered Japan the chance to surrender under their terms and stop war. Japan refused and on 6 August 1945 America reacted by dropping the first nuclear bombs in man's history on Hiroshima and three days later Nagasaki, killing an estimated 437,000 innocent people. On 15 August 1945 the Japanese surrendered and the world war was over.

It is estimated that the war generated a debt with the countries involved, in today's money, of $1,019 billion and took the lives of 54 million soldiers and civilians with most being under the age of 22. The only beneficiaries of the war were the financiers, the world banks, and the suppliers of arms. Germany and Great Britain were both still recovering from the First World War. Where did the money come from for such a campaign? The world bankers or 'World Bangsters' as they are commonly known. Great Britain borrowed an estimated $31.4 billion to finance the war, with interest of course, which took until 2006 to pay back.

THE CORPORATION OF AMERICA

There are three city states that run our world, independent from the countries in which they are based. The world's economy is run through London's inner city 'The City of London Corporation', the world's military is run through the District of Columbia 'The Corporation of America' and spiritually through the Vatican 'The Vatican City State'. The flag of Washington's District of Columbia has three red stars, one for each city state of the empire.

On 17 September 1787 the original constitution for the United States of America was formed establishing the national government and fundamental laws. In 1791, ten amendments were made which are known as the 'Bill of Rights' which were changed giving more freedom to the people in respect to free speech, fair trials and such like. But, when congress passed the Act of 1871 it created a separate corporate government for the District of Columbia. This city state was officially created allowing the District of Columbia to operate as a corporation outside the original constitution of the United States, as a private corporation unattached to the people. The constitution for the District of Columbia operates under a tyrannical Roman law known as Lex Fori, which has no resemblance to the US Constitution.

The President of America is the president of 'The Corporation of America', the elected representative of the independent company who was empowered and allowed to run, by the congress, the American, United States.

A democratic system is where the people vote and the majority wins. The problem with this is that it does not protect the individual person, without rules and a governing body you have no rights over the majority decision. A Republic on the other hand is a system where the rules of the land are clearly stated and the elected representative of the people, with limited power, governs the people.

The government is not there to tell the people what they can and cannot do, like restrict our freedom and individuality. We vote them in to serve us the people to govern our country and uphold the laws of our land.

The ultimate Republic is for the people to vote democratically for their representative but live under a governing republic group which is strictly limited by law of their own powers, leaving freedom for the people and controlling any corruption within the rule. The essence of freedom is the strict limitations of government by the people, once the governing bodies are empowered, the people's freedom always declines.

This is exactly what is happening today, where through devious manipulation of litigation within the banking and governing system and corporate giants, they have deceived the American public and they now hold all financial and governing power, using Columbia as their base.

Britain is as a constitutional monarchy meaning that the Sovereign is Head of State, but the ability to construct and pass legislation resides with an elected parliament and prime minister voted by the people. The British Queen still holds full control over all matters in Great Britain if she desires but the running of the country is left to our electives and has been so since 1707. England did not become a democracy until the 'Representation of the People Act' in 1918 and 1928, allowing men, women and people over the age of 21 to vote. This time in history marked the first major milestone of women's equality, pushed for years by the suffragettes.

The problem with both of these systems is that slowly, unlike a strict republic, laws can be changed to suppress the working people by restricting their freedom and rights, the people have no say in the laws which are passed. Every four years we are allowed to change our leading party by a democratic voting system which stops any party veering to far left or right but the suppressing laws are often left in place. Now that we have voted to leave the clutches and restraints of the European rule we could once again become a great nation with a strong leader and make life free again.

THE AMERICAN WAR BUSINESS

A purported 53% of the revenue produced by human tax in the USA is invested in producing arms and military machinery capable of world destruction. Newly elected President Trump announced this year they would be spending nearly $700 billion on defence, which is nearly as much budget as the rest of the world put together. The country is broke and has been since 1933. It had a deficit of $19.9 trillion back in 2017. The global banks lend revenue to countries using the people as collateral to pay by tax for the debt. The only reason for a country to be in debt is mismanagement, corruption and misuse of funds. Most countries have the resources, if managed correctly, to run without accumulating debt, it is the mismanagement of governing groups always, which brings a country to its knees.

The US Corporation runs war as a business as well as a defence. The war budget is spent on research and producing high technology fighting machinery which is for sale to the highest bidder, all wars need to be supplied. This is not only a defence budget it is a budget for attack for its own gain. Many select private enterprises and corporations, people in the club, earn huge profits from the war industry. War is manufactured as a product of the industry; otherwise there would be no business. All wars are calculated and strategically planned, manufactured to produce wealth and ownership of new land. Sending innocent and vulnerable brainwashed teenagers to lose their lives or be maimed for the good of the country, trained as killing machines, used as dispensable firing fodder.

The latest drain of money is the 'Space Race' a disgusting amount of unnecessary money wasted by top nations on producing destructive laser technology using satellites circling our planet armed ready to destroy each other in what seems to be preparation for the final world war.

The country was spawned from a gene pool of greed brought on by the gold rush and exploitation of human slavery. For such a young country it is by far the most aggressive and intrusive nation on Earth. Since its conception in 1776 it has only seen 21 years of peace in 243 years, without being part of a war.

Has man learnt nothing from its past, are we really that ignorant or is it just the will and greed of the few who run our world. Wars are never wanted by the people it brings nothing but death and destruction. Is it truly the will of the human race to continually fight and declare war on each other and devastate the harmony that we have? Surely a treaty of peace can be achieved throughout the nations without joining as one as this would kill our individual personalities as independent countries and people. The spice of life is diversity. The problems have always arisen from governing groups who wish to force their righteous rules upon the populace instead of representing the people. There must be a time in the near future when we all must make a stand in the name of freedom, come together and unite to protect our rights as humans and protect our mother earth, our only home.

THE VIETNAM WAR

Vietnam in many ways was much more horrific and corrupt than the Second World War. It is a French colony; it was not a war America should have been involved in. President Johnson the head of the USA at the time did not want the communist rule to expand into the south quarters of Vietnam which America had pledged support with defence 11 years before. North and south became divided and with China supplying the north with weapons and bombs North Vietnam invaded south. America sent troops to help train and support southern Vietnam with warships patrolling the nearby seas. North Vietnam shot warning fire at the warships and America's response was to fight back. On August 1964 America invaded North Vietnam in a war which was to last until 1973 for the American soldiers. They pulled out in 1973 defeated by the Japanese and two years later the northern communists won the war. One more triumph for the War profiteers but the death of a decade of young soldiers.

JOHN F KENNEDY

In 1961 on 20 January America witnessed probably their finest president sworn into office John F Kennedy. He was the last president of America who had good intentions of changing the world's corruption in the heartland of where it began. He made a famous speech outlining his proposals for exposing and cutting out the cancer that had already infiltrated the governing bodies of America which had manipulated the amendments to take control of the country's wealth, right under their nose.

Two weeks after his speech on 22 November 1963 he was assassinated.

The New World Order is something very real and has been planned for many years going back to the 17th Century being handed down by the secret societies to achieve their ultimate goal of complete fascist, geographical and financial control over humanity.

Below is Kennedy's speech which guaranteed his elimination, outlining his concerns and full awareness of the corrupt corporation running the country from the shadows pledging to expose them all.

"The very word secrecy is repugnant in a free and open society and we are as a people inherently and historically opposed to secret societies, to secret oaths and to secret proceedings. We decided long ago that the dangers of excessive and unwarranted concealment of pertinent facts far outweighed the dangers which are cited to justify it.

Even today there is little value in opposing the threat of a closed society by imitating its arbitrary restrictions. Even today there is little value in ensuring the survival of our nation if our traditions do not survive with it. And there is very grave danger that an unannounced need for increased security will be seized upon by those anxious to expand its meaning to the very limits of official censorship and concealment. That I do not intend to permit to the extent that it's my control and no official of my administration whether his rank is high or low, civilian or military should interpret my words here tonight as an excuse to censor the news to stifle dissent to cover up our mistakes or to withhold from the press and the public the facts they desire to know, for we are opposed around the world by a monolithic and ruthless conspiracy that relies primarily on covert means for expanding its sphere of influence on infiltration instead of invasion on submersion instead of elections on intimidation instead of free choice on guerrilla's by night instead of armies by day. It is a system which has conscripted vast human and material resources into the building of a tightly knit, highly efficient machine that combines military, diplomatic, intelligence, economic, scientific and political operations. Its preparations are concealed not published. Its mistakes are buried not headlined. Its dissenters are silenced not praised, no expenditure is questioned no rumour is printed, no secret is revealed. No president should fear public scrutiny of his program for from that scrutiny comes understanding and from that understanding comes support or opposition and both are necessary. I am not asking your newspapers to support an administration but I am asking your help in the tremendous task of informing and alerting the American people for I have complete confidence in the response and dedication of our citizens whenever they are fully informed. I not only could stifle controversy among your readers I welcome it. This administration intends to be candid about its errors, for a wise man once said; an error doesn't become a mistake until you refuse to correct it. We intend to accept full responsibility for our errors and we expect you to point them out when we miss them without debate, without criticism, no administration and no country can succeed and no republic can survive. That is why the Athenian law maker Solon decreed a crime for any citizen to shrink from controversy and that is why our press was protected by the first amendment the only business in America specially protected by the constitution, not primarily to amuse and entertain not to emphasize the trivial and the sentimental not to simply give the public what it wants but to inform to arouse to reflect to state our dangers and our opportunities to indicate our crises and our choices to lead morally educate and sometimes even anger public opinion. This means greater coverage and analysis of international news for it is no longer far away and foreign but close at hand and local. It means greater attention to improved understanding of the news as well as improved transmission. And it means finally that the government at all levels must meet its obligation to provide you with the fullest possible information outside the narrowest limits of national security. And so it is the printing press to the recorder of man's deeds, the keeper of his conscience the courier of his news that we look for strength and assistance, I am confident that with your help man will be what he was born to be, free and independent".

"There is a plot in this country to enslave every man woman and child. Before I leave this high and noble office I intend to expose this plot"

Shortly before his assassination on 4 June 1963 he signed an executive order to end the Federal Reserve. The politics of why and who he was going to expose goes much deeper but the end result was the same, he was murdered.

GADDAFI'S MURDER

Muhammad Gaddafi was the leader of Libya, North Africa for 40 years, one of the longest reigns recorded. Contrary to media coverage his people respected his rule as he brought many favourable benefits for the people. He constructed one of the biggest water irrigation systems in the world in the desert sands so that the people could farm, grow and prosper bringing life and commerce to the dead lands. He himself spent much of his time living in a tabernacle not a huge palace. His own people were allowed to use the new irrigated lands free of charge to start the project running. He gave free healthcare to his country which in Africa was a golden gift. They had the highest results in education throughout Africa for free, cheap petrol and affordable living. He published 'The Green Book' in 1975 explaining to his people his intentions of rule and future projects for the country, he was a good and competent leader. His style of rule was different from the west which attracted much criticism but it is a different system with different morals and religious beliefs engrained for centuries in this kind of culture, they had no right to interfere and disable the country and eliminate the leader.

The whole story and propaganda generated by the media of the demise and brutal murder of Muhammad Gaddafi on world network news was a complete fabrication. Shortly before the travesty of Gaddafi he met with the leaders of the Arab world proposing that the oil was to be traded in 'Dinar' instead of American dollars. This action if it had been implemented would have destroyed the American dollar and empowered the African and Arab people with the world bankers losing control of trade in oil with the American dollar. Africa has been suppressed for years with embargoes and trade suppression, this was not an option for the world leaders to allow to happen so he was wiped out.

CHAPTER 5

THE IMPLICATIONS OF DISASTER

One of the biggest threats to mankind today is the pollution of our seas and food chain. The people who invented napalm in the Vietnam War 'Monsanto' the makers of death and destruction are slowly taking over the monopoly of our food crops worldwide. In the 1970s pesticides started to be commonly used for insect and weed control alongside food crops in Europe and the USA. Which genius decided growing our food with poisons was a good idea? The whole concept is ludicrous and is a worldwide disaster waiting to happen. It is the only product name I know which works very hard and pays vast amounts of money to keep their name off their food products rather than promote them. This in itself must give you an indication that genetically modified organisms (GMO), rightly nicknamed 'The Seeds of Death' is highly dangerous for our future and most definitely not to be consumed.

Genetically modified crops are grown in many countries around the world, while 30 nations have prohibited their cultivation. In 2015 most European nations decided to block the cultivation of GMOs within their country and Russia issuing a complete ban on both cultivation and importation. Monsanto is the company that told us that Polychlorinated Biphenyls were safe to be used in lubricants and coolants from 1935-1977 although these toxic chemicals caused human harm and environmental pollution affecting whole villages in the US who worked at these plants. Agent Orange was one of their products used in the Vietnam War as part of its herbicidal warfare program. Today they are quickly gaining the monopoly on our food chain. Monsanto's job is to make money for their investors and have global control of all food stocks. It is blatant that they have no concern for the environmental carnage or side effects to our health.

The corrupt system is very simple, owning the rights to the seeds and the rights to grow the seeds on your land. Monsanto patented the rights to sell their modified seed which has been made genetically barren so that each year new seeds must be bought from Monsanto and no other seed by law can be grown on your land. For centuries farms all round the world have been handed down father to son using the grain for next year's crop quite happily and successfully. Monsanto claims that the modified seeds will produce a higher yield and larger produce, greater than natural seeds can attain. By signing the contract they have given up the rights of their land forever and become working caretakers of what was theirs in the first place. Owning all the food producing land by manipulative contract of the world is their quest, control of what we eat. These seeds are now patented property of one corporation, Monsanto. If you have an organic crop that sits next to a genetically engineered field you will get cross pollination and your organic crop will be irreversibly poisoned. If you grow your next year's crop with the contaminated seed Monsanto can take you to court, growing their crop out of contract. In Canada there are groups of farmers fighting for their land back after their experiences with these evil capitalists.

Independent studies conducted on the impact of genetically modified food on our bodies shows that it can damage organs and cause infertility. It is an unnatural product which affects the immune system which can lead to cancers and growths. It causes unnecessary irritation to our whole digestive system. It is wrong and is criminal to interfere with our basic food needs.

The effect on the world's natural growth system will be devastating, it is interfering with the very basic fundamental need of all of us, all in the name of greed and power. The knock on effect is already apparent, it will destroy and replace nature's own self seeding process that has served us well for thousands of years, killing off the insects which pollinate our crops and play such an important part in the food cycle. Killing off pollinating bees and other vital insects that break down the waste and soils in our fields and also in turn provide food for other creatures. One of the concerns of food experts is that the poisons/insecticides used for our food growth, whether it be GMO or not, is killing the nutriments and minerals in the very soil in which it is grown so we are producing and eating non-nutritional food which does not keep our immune system to a level of safety and well-being. In short, grow your own with natural seed or buy and eat organic. England has a chance as an island to grow organic food and feed its people without the crops being cross pollinated or poisoned by GMOs 'seeds of death'.

In England if a GMO ingredient is in a food product, for example bread, it does not need to be declared on the label as it is not the finished product and so the origin of the ingredients are unknown to the consumer. It often states on processed foods, these being the worst offenders of undesirable ingredients, 'processed and packed in the UK' no indication of product origin or possible GMO products, the laws and regulations must be changed for our protection.

Although most of Europe, except parts of Spain, does not cultivate GMO foods, it is still one of the world's biggest consumers of them and most European countries still import GMO products. Biotech corn and soy are used to feed our cattle, and in turn we eat that meat and still drink the milk and dairy products produced by these animals but still wonder why breast cancer and other related cell mutations are rife in our society. Have we already forgotten the 'Mad Cow Disease' episode, how human consumption of misfed livestock has a direct impact on our health and immune system? It is the body's immune system itself due to lack of minerals and build up of toxins through pesticides that allows growths and cancer cells to form. The intake of chemical poisons from food or liquid or inhaling toxins or radiation overwhelms your body's immune system and this causes illness. Choose your food wisely or face the consequences, we do not have to eat contaminated food and we must boycott GMO at all costs before it devastates the world's food chain.

The Public Record Office in London is a vast national archive of documents covering the last 1,000 years of British history. At the beginning of each year it is possible to gain government papers which have been kept secret from the public domain for 25 years under Britain's Public Records Act. (If a record is judged to be too sensitive by our government department then it can apply to extend public viewing for a period up to one hundred years). In 2002 the Observer paper, following investigations into released documents, published an article concerning undeclared chemical experiments on the British people. The Ministry of Defence turned parts of the English countryside into a giant laboratory to conduct a series of secret germ warfare experiments on the unsuspecting public of England using gasses dispersed by planes. The government reports give a detailed comprehensive history of these barbaric actions of biological weapon trials between 1940 and 1979. There are several documentaries showing accounts of whole families who have died through cancer directly associated with these experiments. America has numerous reports also of the same findings with accounts of misuse of chemicals causing cancerous and fatal casualties. We are tax earning cattle and are treated as animals.

Mounting evidence from around the world suggests that millions of tons of aluminium, barium and strontium are used in geo-engineering by governments to alter the atmosphere for purposes that are still unclear. Scientists in several countries have linked recent unexplained mass animal and sea mammal's deaths with aluminium and barium toxins, drawing even more attention to global experiments.

Many scientists believe aluminium is linked with Alzheimer's Disease and is known as a neurotoxin, with mounting evidence that chronic exposure is a factor in many neurological diseases, including dementia, autism and Parkinson's disease. Lobbyists worldwide are protesting about the contrails, the use of commercial planes purported to be spraying these substances, although nothing is being achieved except awareness.

JAPAN

In the North Pacific sea there is a vast area which is named 'The Ring of Fire' where many of the world's tectonic plates meet, this produces volcanoes where the earth's crust meets and breathes. Earthquakes are frequent and volcanic eruptions common although mostly small. The Ring of Fire was named because of the positioning of the volcanoes which are situated in a large circle surrounding the North Pacific region. People living in these areas are fully aware of the dangers and choose to live life with their possible fate.

China and America within the ring, have a huge land mass of usable space, it is only that people cluster and tend to dwell in big cities or close to busy sea ports that it seems the world is over populated.

Around the world there are over 400 nuclear power stations in 31 different countries and some are built directly on known tectonic plate lines in the Pacific region. In Fukushima, Japan, their power station had a meltdown after an earthquake some five years ago and the world sits around pointing the finger and does nothing to help. They are built near the sea for cooling purposes but when they malfunction like Fukushima, it pollutes and continues to pollute vast sections of the world's seas and corals. If this energy must still be used at least build the plant inland and pump the water to the plant and have a safety plan. If the world really was run by people who truly care about our planet, as they tell us, surely they should help Japan to clear this environmental ongoing poisoning of the Pacific sea. Four hundred and fifty gallons of nuclear waste is flushing in to the Pacific daily. Seventy five percent of all coral is reported to have been destroyed in the surrounding seas. The West Coast of America is now showing signs of contamination in the sea and air, and many fish from these seas are showing signs of contamination and will soon be marked as unfit for human consumption, and yet no one is helping Japan.

Nuclear energy is outdated, it is highly dangerous and yet still used and the toxic waste products stay active for hundreds of years, what a legacy to leave our next generation.

Forget the woes and corruption of the ruling class for a moment and let us take stock of our situation as a race of people. There are some dynamic people who shine through the fog and lead the way in different avenues of new technology working for a cleaner, better future for the planet but whether they will be allowed to succeed, the near future will tell.

NIKOLA TESLA

Nikola Tesla was a man born ahead of his time, the forgotten genius of the last century and only now is his work being used and recognised in the bid for clean and free energy. He was born in Yugoslavia but moved to America hoping to be able to finance his obsession with inventions and ideas of producing free electricity for the world's masses. He was a humanist.

He held 700 patents with the most famous being the 'Alternating Current' or AC electrical current which we all use today. This man was responsible for producing the first commercial electric lighting system which soon replaced the gas lamps. He had to fight his rival Thomas Edison, an American capitalist who tried to establish his own idea of DC current system, but DC was proved to be too dangerous for public use. Tesla went on to build the first hydroelectric power plant at Niagara Falls which harnessed the natural flow of water producing power via turbines, enough to illuminate the whole town of Buffalo USA on 16 November 1896, but alas the dream of free power to the common people was squashed. He invented the x-ray which completely changed our health industry and understanding of the human body. Radio waves, fluorescent tubes, bulbs with no cables and the list goes on. He eventually died a poor man, all his work for the good of humanity unless it could earn money for the investors, was squashed and the patents where refused and ridiculed.

At the time of Tesla's death the American government entered his apartment and confiscated all his papers and designs.

The ruling and world investment class had invested heavily in fossil fuels, the coal and the new petroleum industry, they were not going to allow the masses to have free power, god forbid helping the working class people. Tesla was outcast by investors through media slander campaigns and he never fully recovered.

The most famous of his inventions was 'Warden Cliff Towers' a huge domed tower which was constructed to attract natural electric current, direct from the earth's ionosphere which would produce thousands of volts of free energy. JP Morgan, one of the original pioneer Bankers of America who first invested in the construction, soon put a stop to all investors involved as soon as the idea of free wireless lighting was implied. The tower was later decommissioned and blown to bits with dynamite.

It is suggested that by the year 2055 if the trend and demand for petroleum continues with the population growth as today, the supply will not be able to meet the demand. The technology of clean power to turn the gears of society is already here, to run the grid systems of the world, to run our cars and trains but it still is not being used. Many wealthy investors choose money over sense and worldly self gain.

Electric cars dependant on batteries is not the answer for future transport, it is just another phase. Mining and refining Lithium, the material used to store electricity will cause just as much carnage in the environment as oil. If the worlds populous all drove vehicles fuelled by electric, the power grids would not be able to cope. Within the next 20 years, if allowed, the cogs of power will be run by the very same principle of earth itself, fuel free and emission free. The technology is already here but because of vast investments in the oil industry it will take another 30 years to evolve. It will not be allowed until the oil fields are dry.

CHAPTER 6

OUR FUTURE

In 1969 we put a man on the moon, although debated, and later introduced the computer to the world. Since then we have been probing space and preparing for the next generation of 3D printing and robotic run factories. But as technology accelerates at a speed unknown to us before, we should be coming together as a race of people not draining vital resources and fighting each other still. We have more pressing appointments that need immediate attention. It is predicted that in 2029 we have a meteor heading our way with the potential of wiping out a large portion of humanity and rendering the planet's surface uninhabitable for some years. Instead of spending billions of dollars on 'particle beam' weapons floating around in our orbit pointing them at our fellow man in preparation for World War 3, how about peace and trying to live in harmony, stop the aggression and work together but still, as independent countries.

The 'particle beam' weapon was invented by Nicola Tesla in 1934, a weapon that was estimated to be capable of destroying whole military bases in one quick process at a distance of 250 miles. Tesla gave America, Russia, Canada and England all separate pieces of the same design plan so that no single country could own such a destructive weapon. The idea was for all countries to unite in peace instead of world destruction. But the space war which is happening now has laser systems similar to Tesla's design. I find it all very sad. The American corporation will be remembered in years to come as the greedy people, the snake who knowingly ate his own tail.

Within the next hundred years the world's technology will surpass the ability of human capability. Robotics will take centre stage with all commercial mass production of commerce. Three million commercial robotic systems are already in use in the world today slowly rendering the human workforce obsolete. A company today in Boston USA is producing free moving robotics for military use in the fighting fields with prototypes moving as fast as humans over rough terrain using hydraulic systems with unbelievable results. In Japan they are mastering the art of trans-humanism making clones of people as robots with incredible accuracy with the humanoids able to have conversations independently without human interaction and having thoughts and making decision by themselves. The Tesla car company run by Elon Musk is suggesting they will be sending rockets to Mars within the next ten years with the intention of changing the atmosphere of the planet with nuclear fusion to render the planet habitable. The robotic humanoids will play a big part in these processes and no doubt mining for precious metals as well.

With the new technology of quantum computer systems the hardware is becoming ever smaller and gaining speed at an alarming rate. Although the software is dragging its feet compared with the hardware, virtual reality and design programs in four dimensional aspects are accelerating in a direction of unimaginable proportions.

We invented the computer some 60 years ago as our own biological memory and capabilities were becoming inadequate for the demands of our imagination and quickly accelerating evolution. It has now reached a stage where we have created perhaps a monster which needs feeding. To keep pushing forward as a race, which is our human instinct, it appears that we will need to adapt our body and mind, to perfect the human body to cope with the new industrial revolution which is looming, and become hybrids, half human, part machine. Although we have this technology do we really need to use it, do we have to take all known technology to the extreme? Artificial intelligence or simply AI as it is known will be so overpowering and constrictive to the human race and in the wrong hands, devastating. The introduction of 5G high frequency technology which is rapidly being set up in America will show the rest of the world how manipulative and controlling this new technology will be, it will be the end of human freedom and privacy.

We will experience wars using robotic armies and unmanned fighter jets being directed and played out from across the world in the comfort of a swivel chair like an animated PC game and the use of 'Slaughter Bolt' drones, small programmable flying devices designed purely for the purpose to kill, directed straight to your mobile phone via satellite navigation.

The art of connecting hardware to the human brain is already in our grasp: when this is perfected people will be able to upload data direct to their internal processor via blue tooth or future systems. Projective imagery is also now available with fantasy games or data being able to be projected on to a contact lens in your eye at will. Hard to imagine perhaps but if you were offered a perfect memory which has access to all the known data in the world would you pass it by and refuse. Technology is fuelled by demand, investment and control, the financial implications of trans-humanism is enormous. Research in many useful fields is often ignored, as the end result will not be profitable, even if it benefits mankind.

Phones will be a thing of the past, just another cleverly marketed product to feed on the masses, preparing the new generation for the ultimate goal. The new system will be within the body using nano quantum chips, processors and receivers. Scientists now are working on programmable viruses, micro-organisms which can be inhaled and transmitted through the air or injected as nano microbes to help fight cancers and such like, so we are told. One can only admire the genius, imagination and insight of those who study and produce results in this field. But in the wrong hands this technology will be catastrophic in ways I try not to think about. The fusion of atoms was turned into the atom bomb, Nikola Tesla's particle beam laser is now a weapon of war, what will they do with programmable viruses. If you wish to wipe out the populous of a country, program a virus. Once control of our inner selves is established we have no hope. Choose wisely before allowing your child or yourself to be impregnated with a virus or any other vaccine they wish to violate our bodies with.

We are at the stage of technology now where experiments are being carried out involving the actual changing of the atom structure. Similar to the 3D printer, but feeding in base elements of nature's building blocks like carbon and other minerals and programming the machine to make a living creature, at this stage we will be playing god, but with no instructions.

In 400 years time I fear we will lose all connection with nature and we may not recognize ourselves, if we are still alive.

If the passion, enthusiasm and finance used to create war was diverted to repairing and restructuring our planet, there would be a chance of a clean prosperous future for mankind. Already with some aspects of nature ecologically we have crossed the line of no return. Scientists estimate that 150-200 species of plant, insect, bird and mammal become extinct every 24 hours accelerated by our mismanagement of Earth. The lungs of the planet, our trees, are being cut down and not replenished at a dangerously critical rate. Our seas from which we feed are becoming polluted by our discarded waste and nuclear leakage poisoning whole areas. If nothing is done with immediate affect we truly have a problem. Gold is worthless if we cannot eat or breathe.

There have been many civilisations before us, everything repeats in cycles. My belief is that we are travelling a road that we have already walked. Many civilisations before us have fallen, let us not be the next.

THE ATLANTA GUIDER STONES

In the town of Elberton, Georgia USA stands a huge granite monument described as a 'small Stone Henge' built in 1980. It lies on the outskirts of the town and is highly protected and maintained by the local sheriff with 24-hour surveillance cameras, although the owners and designers of the slabs, when investigated, seem to be unknown.

On the tall towering slabs of granite is written, carved in stone in eight different world languages, the agenda for the 'New World Order'. It states quite clearly carved out of stone like the ten Commandments, a series of actions which will be enforced upon the human population.

First: Depopulation of humanity to 500 million people (world gencide of 80% of humans)

Second: One world rule, with one world court (one dictating power group running the world)

Third: Enforced birth control to keep the population steady (selective breeding)

Fourth: One world language with one world religion (one united religious control)

Fifth: Balance personal rights with social duties (slavery)

You must come to your own conclusion when examining such blatant facts although most information concerning the New World Control quite clearly shows we are dealing with a small but powerful group of monstrous individuals.

Remembering this dream, or nightmare, has been planned for hundreds of years and handed down the families of the ruling class, now is the era they will try to enforce these polices of depopulation and mass control.

Thirty years in the future there will be little use for 'human livestock', we will be a liability and more importantly for them, an unnecessary cost. 3D printing machines and robot alternative production lines are already replacing human function; they produce 24 hours a day without a tea break. It is efficient and it is used now today. Houses, bridges, all structures can be made with little human interaction bar one programmer. Will the redundant people of the world be paid a wage as suggested for nothing by the fat cats with no restrictions, I think not.

On 11 September 1991 George H W Bush stated live in a public speech to the US nation his plans to dominate and rule the world as one governing body. In his own words he announced "A new world order and when we succeed, and we will, the whole world will be run by one governing group of leaders". The declaration of 'The New World Order'.

DENVER NEW WORLD AIRPORT

A controversial airport in Denver, USA was constructed in 1994 which was named 'Denver New World Airport'. A plaque in the form of a capstone was laid for the opening of the airport stating that the American Masonic Fraternity of the USA had designed and built the structure. The plaque is carved with the traditional 'dividers and set square' one of the symbols of the Masonic Lodge and a time capsule was planted to be opened in 2094. It is one of the first airports with vast underground connecting tunnels and mass storage.

An artist was commissioned to paint and create a sculpture for the airport of the Masons design.   On entering the airport you are greeted with a huge bronze black demonic looking horse rearing up in a fighting stance with luminous red eyes. Nearing the end of the commission after the paintings had been finished a freak accident occurred where a section of the bronze horse fell on the artist and killed him outright, an accident they claimed.

Artist Luis Jimenez painted, as commissioned, scenes of the near future of our world in a series of canvasses which are hung in the main hall. The first reveals scenes of horrific chemical warfare with mothers and children crying with dead bodies scattered around after a worldwide genocidal apocalypse, the aftermath of depopulation of the planet. Depictions of Hitler's perfect race ideal of ridding the world of the genetically weak, disabled and poor people held by Hitler and carried still. The other paintings show how the world's people were tricked and betrayed showing the polluted aftermath of the depopulation of man. People wearing gas masks amongst the debris of broken buildings and how the remaining populace is suppressed and kept in order by militarised new age cops.

Not really my choice of ideal airport art décor to ease passengers just before a flight. You could not make this up, symbolic fresco like depictions of our demise; the whole episode is very bizarre and causes much controversy amongst locals and visitors alike.

911

The 911 Twin Towers attack in America will go down in history as the worst thought out 'false flag' incident in the 21st century, although you must come to your own conclusion. If I was investigating the case the truth is plain and simple to see. The inside beneficiaries who had prior warning of the event who earned vast amounts of profit on the stock market the following day and the amended insurance contract made prior to the disaster is where the investigation stops. The physical details of a 1,362 ft steel tower building, being hit sideways by a 306-ton commercial airliner and then being raised to the ground vertically without a flinch of movement left or right, without the aid of explosives or electro wave technology is preposterous. But alas no one will be brought to justice for this horrific crime forced upon its own people. It was executed to start a war on another unsuspecting country to destabilise and control a new section of the world. The event gained the confidence of the people through the media coverage allowing another war on another country to go ahead. Over 2,900 of their own people died that day. This is not the first or the last time these sick events will happen; think twice when listening to your biased news.

WHAT IS THE HUMAN RACE?

Understanding and accepting what we are in the eyes of science is challenging and uncomfortable for some to comprehend. The origins of our biology start from bacteria which was brought to this planet billions of years ago by a meteor from other parts of space.

Light and sound travels through our surrounding air or space both at different speeds. Whilst observing a lightning and thunder storm the light appears first and the sound after. Light travels faster than sound and the time difference between the two equates to how far away the storm is. On a larger scale, the stars we see in space are thousands of light years away; these stars may not exist anymore as the light has taken thousands of years to reach us by wavelength from the original source. Depending on the strength of the light, the light continues to move by wave after the death of a star or other light source. If you drop a stone in a still lake the splash creates circular waves travelling outwards, this phenomenon is the same for light and sound, the waves continue after the stone has sunk. Light from the sun takes eight minutes before it reaches earth for the same reason, travelling as a wave.

We as humans are conscious beings living inside a body of matter. Our soul, our true being our thinking, conscious selves are a separate entity to the physical body we rent in this world. All structured matter is made of atoms, mostly hydrogen, nitrogen and oxygen with carbon being the basic building blocks. These atoms come together in the same process that the planets were formed. Gravity pulls the atoms together forming a solid state, as our bodies are now. For our bodies to stay in this form we have a constant wavelength pushing against us in all directions in the form of pressure and the same for all living things. This pressure is kept constant on Earth by the magnetic field and ionosphere. A wavelength or force produced by its iron and nickel core produces a magnetic field which also protects us from the sun's atomic rays, keeping our world stable. The earth is a huge natural generator of electricity with a highly complex system of self-preservation. If we travel to space unprotected this wave is lost and our body returns to atoms and ceases to hold its form.

The final conclusion to date of the beginning of the universe put forward by physicists is the theory of 'The Big Bang'. I believe this theory is no theory at all, just an explanation of an event that takes place within our universe not the answer to the original creation. If hydrogen and helium atoms caused a thermo nuclear fusion and exploded outwards creating the universe as they suggest, you must ask, what is the explosion travelling into, more space? Who created that space? And what formed the atoms in the beginning? So the question of genesis still remains.

Science tells us that every action has an equal reaction. If the Big Bang Theory, an explosion, is travelling outwards in all directions there must have already been a force equal to that force allowing the reaction to happen? Their explanation of the Big Bang Theory suggests, because of the law of gravity the universe created itself 'spontaneous creation', it was created from nothing, I am unconvinced. Nothing is created from nothing especially if the art of creation itself, did not exist at this time.

We must accept for now, which is beyond our comprehension, that the universe with which our planets and galaxies are formed is infinite, it has no beginning or end. We are a nano phenomena floating in an eternal mist of intrigue.

The true original creator of our life as humans is our sun. At the end of a star's life, if it has a big enough mass, it eventually explodes giving into the force of gravity creating a huge outward explosive wave called a nebula. A nebula is a spinning cloud of gas and dust. When the gas and dust collect at the centre of the nebula, a Protostar is formed. When the Protostar is large enough, nuclear fusion begins within the gasses and the star starts to burn and shine. This forms a new galaxy with the possibility of new life. Our small cluster of planets, is that creation, we owe our life to our sun.

If the sun's mass is too small when the hydrogen is depleted, it eventually becomes a white dwarf and slowly fades out never giving birth to a new galaxy again. If the sun is of huge mass it ends its life becoming a supernova which creates a massive laser of light and power which thrusts out of its centre into space and eventually becomes a black hole, although we have no evidence and can only theorise.

We invented time to structure our lives along with the cycle of the sun and the moon. We created history on our planet so we have key points of reference. Space on the other hand has no known start or finish and we have no other reference to compare the size of space or our existence too. So we created a god and heaven so we knew where we were heading and created a theory of the universe to keep us content.

The body is made up of 80% water, along with oxygen, hydrogen, nitrogen, calcium, phosphorus and carbon the building material. The sun is made of mostly hydrogen and helium, carbon and trace elements. We are made of the same elements as the sun; all of nature is connected although we have sadly forgotten this concept. Seventy-five per cent of our galaxy is just hydrogen which holds memory, the same as water, scientists suggest that all the history of the universe is held in the universal biological memory.

Our body itself is a huge receptor, a receiver of information made up of trillions of atoms working independently but connected as a whole like the nervous system used with touch and feel. Our body reacts to all outside change environmentally and consciously through wavelengths picked up through our five senses; this is our only means of knowing we are alive. The body is made up of atoms which are 99% empty consisting of a minute nucleus and electrons. The body is mostly water, so we are a conscious spirit separate from the body, inside a piece of matter held together by a constant wave of force. Consciousness travels faster than light. The origin of the force which relays the wave is the biggest question.

All of nature on earth is connected with the sun and the geometry of the greater universe. The universe itself sends our wave, we are the wave of consciousness being received by our body, and at the time of our body's demise we return to the mass of energy in a conscious state of spirit. Everything is constantly moving in the universe even when we are in a state of motionless silence.

"All matter originates and exists only as a virtue of a force, we must assume behind this force is the existence of a conscious and intelligent mind, this mind is the matrix of all matter". Max Planck, the father of quantum physics 1858-1947 (Ref/Sec 8).

In 1975 Benoit Mandelbrot discovered a fractal phenomenon which is known as the fingerprint of god and named 'The Mandelbrot set'. It is the simplified explanation of our position, understanding and essence of our existence. Whilst looking into a microscope at any piece of nature or material mater, you will discover a new biological world of living microbes and organisms. Look deeper and you will find another micro world within that world and so on. We on this planet are at the end of someone else's microscope, and at the end of that microscope is another looking down on him, like the Russian dolls that fit inside each other. The universe is a never-ending minimisation or magnification in all directions being part of different layers of worlds but different sizes. The Mandelbrot is presented as the Vesica Piscis of nature, the mathematical structure of the world. But it explains in my view that factually we have no proven knowledge of our size or position as the universe has no end or no beginning; it's a mass of infinite levels, we are part of the Mandelbrot of the universe. (Ref. Sec.2)

"You are not a drop in the ocean, you are the ocean as a drop "(Remi, 13th century Poet), we are connected and come from the same source of energy, we came from there and we will return there as a conscious being, energy does not die it just transforms.

The future is not here yet, the past no longer exists, and the present takes up no time at all. We are in an ordered accelerating path of history merely skimming the present time like a blink of an eye. Your perception of now is already in the past, our present time is very short, life is for living, live it well.

Without freedom for the people we have no diversity, with no diversity there is no life.

WHAT THE NEAR FUTURE HOLDS AND THE DIRECT IMPLICATIONS FOR YOU

The near future does not need to be grim it depends on how we all react to the demands of the NWO and their new suppressive delights that they wish to force upon us. The new world agenda is all about controlling and regimenting the masses which is nothing new but technology available today, allows forced control of taxation and automated penalty systems to be undertaken and enforced via the web, automatically with no or little human interaction. All transactions and law will soon be made via the web on one world central computer.

One world central bank will own all other subsidiary banks with all transactions going through one set of worldly accounts. All financial transactions will eventually be conducted through your body chip or personal swipe system and all cash will be abolished controlling 100% of the economy worldwide. This will rule out any casual transactions, descending into financial slavery with sanctions and taxes. High street banks will eventually become obsolete and be a thing of the past.

Full observational camera systems will be placed on every street and in-house daily items like televisions and smart meters will be fitted with monitor systems to pry and record your private world. It will become an alternated system run on fear and financial control with fingerprint recognition on all web connections and financial transactions.

The Human Rights Bill will be abolished giving the people the same rights as an animal as it was prior to 1948 in UK, this already has been the dream of the Conservative rule for many years.

The divide between rich and poor will expand once more returning to Victorian times experiencing vast poverty and hardship resulting in rulers and workers abolishing the middle class. Central London will continue to house the elite and continue to be the world trade centre; a capital state unconcerned with its country's populous.

It is predicted that if Europe succeeds, they will try to enforce implants into new born babies, whether it is through micro vaccines or chip implants, all humans will be tracked and logged 24 hours a day. It will be brought in through security measures telling us it is for our own safety and security against terrorism. A system was enforced by law in April 2016 in UK for all dogs to be chipped by their owners or a penalty of £500 fine, this is the prototype for ourselves. Human microchip will render any non-conformist unable to travel or purchase any goods forcing the system upon us; we will have no choice if we accept the system. We are approaching a world where our lives will be run by one master dictatorship enforced by military. We are willingly buying into this system through purchasing phone swipe systems and accepting quick payment options, cash will be abolished if we continue to conform.

Forced birth control using genetics in food supplies and vaccines, targeting areas of the world deemed undesirable. Genetic elimination through sterilisation, people considered unfit to live by the ruling class.

Centralised control of all foreign and domestic policies, forcing one world rule upon us all. All commerce and industries are to be the property of the world rule. (Agenda 21)

Reintroduction of conscription in Europe preparing for the war ahead.

With the use of NATO and the UN they will govern and militarise the new ruling of the world order. Armed street police in England will become normality.

As the media and entertainment industries are owned by these people nothing you see or hear can be taken as gospel, today's media world is truly a fabricated stage.

Three super powers hold the nuclear arsenal to obliterate the world as we know it today. By having individual countries it prevents one world rule. If two join forces the other will fall. Let all nations come together as individual countries and live in peace dealing with the world's crises as a whole but as independent nations, is that too much to ask? If the New World Agenda is realised and one power rules Earth there will be no other force to stop that dictatorship. We need diversity in countries and people, in the name of humanity and the freedom of creation, this makes our societies worth living in, being individual from each other.

Europe was formed initially, so we were told, to bring countries together following the Second World War hoping that it would bring peace and unity to the member countries, the opposite in fact is true. To invade 28 different countries with false flags is quite a task, so invade quietly through the back door with contract and pen gaining control anonymously. The blueprint of world domination has not changed as it is the same families leading the same quest. Destabilise the countries, take away the ruling power and leave the country in huge debt leaving them powerless and controlled. Europe is no different; the Trojan horse has already walked through the gates.

On 23 June 2016 a referendum was held for the people of 'The United Kingdom of Great Britain and Northern Ireland' to vote to stay or leave the 'European Union'. The people of England prior to 1973 when we joined the Euro, owned and controlled our own country and surrounding seas. We had a democratic system which empowered the people, to choose by vote, who runs our country and who makes the law. Back in the Second World War our grandfathers gave their lives to protect our freedom and self-rule over our own country, did they fight in vain? By leaving the European Union the British people will regain England once more and the freedom to rule our own country. It is our land, our seas, why would 'free' people, pay vast amounts of revenue, willingly (amounting to £19.5 billion per annum) to a bureaucratic system of dictators to rule us, it is absurd. Through the power of these bureaucrats a second referendum may be implemented to try and influence by media the decision of the British people. If this goes ahead you must be fully aware of the implications.

EU countries are bound to the laws made by the European Committee. The people of Europe have no rights to vote for who is in power or any rights over what laws are passed by the union. We will lose total control over our own destiny and liberty. We relinquish all rights as British people to any laws forced upon us, this is a dictatorship, we are going backwards. It wasn't until 1918 that all men over 21 and women over 30 we were given rights to vote and have some influence over what happened in our country, let us not relinquish these rights now.

Eventually, if the EU succeeds, the member countries will lose their former individual titles and sovereignty and will become simply 'The United European Union', this is the agenda. Migration quotas will be forced upon the EU countries, Europe will experience civil war and upheaval over the next 20 years completely shredding any ounce of its individuality and former self, being controlled by shadow governors who they do not even know. It is an invasion of Europe with the agenda of full financial control, made possible by manipulative, bureaucratic litigation and contract.

Eventually in the Middle East within the next 30 years as the oil fields start to deplete and the world begins to use alternative energy to fuel transportation, Israel will become a capital state, run by the Zionist Jews acting as a central military base in the Middle East. The Sacred Temple on the mount in Jerusalem will be replaced and rebuilt to honour the prophecy of the Jews and await the return of the Anunnaki our creators, or in their gospel, the one true god. On his return, the Jews believe he will rule the world once more from the holy dome in Jerusalem seated on his throne, the 'Ark of the covenant'. He will share the holy lands with his chosen people, the Jews, the only people given divine Covenant from god, as they believe. For this event to happen World War 3 will have to commence in the name of religion completely changing the world as we know it today. This is the prophecy of the Jewish people. The third World War will start in the Middle East.

"As long as there are prisons, police armies and navies we are not civilized. When the earth joins together and uses the earth intelligently, that will be the beginning of civilisation." Jacque Fresco (Ref. Sec. 6)

We consider ourselves to be top of the food chain enslaving and slaughtering innocent animals for our own consumption as we consider them to be below us, with no feelings or intelligence. Perhaps we have been imprisoned ourselves in the same way, positioned on a huge global farm in the corner of space which is impossible to escape, made by a superior advanced race. Taught to collect gold and multiply until the heard is fat, then, return and harvest the crop. I hope for our sake if the Anunnaki are returning as written in the Sumerian tablets, they are not as beastly as us and they are all vegetarians! Or perhaps they are already here?

CHAPTER 7

THE SECRETS OF ALCHEMY AND HERMETIC PHILOSOPHY

Hermetic philosophy and alchemy is the oldest known form of secret doctrine given to mankind in the beginning of our creation thousands of years before the Great Flood in the old times. The true master and watcher of humanity was Thoth known to the Greeks as Hermes Trismegistus. The wisdom of Thoth has been handed down the centuries to the chosen initiates being originally the Egyptians and later Sumerian kings. He taught and guided mankind and he was the carrier of divine messages and recorded all human deeds for the ruling gods.

Gnosticism, Hermeticism and the Kabbalah were all thought to have been brought over to the west by the Knights Templar in the 1200s after their crusades. The god of fertility and nature Baphomet, similar to the Greek god Pan, is often used as the symbol of the devil and death in contemporary cults. One of the first depictions of Baphomet in Europe was sculpted by the Templars on the outside of the 'Notre-Dame' De Paris Cathedral which was originally built by them. As often in history there are many conflicting theories of the gods as each country had their own believes and name for the same god. Most of these gods were from before the flood and later worshipped like Baphomet in contemporary times changing the image to an evil connotation. Elphius Levi in the 1800s a leading French occultist suggests Baphomet was the father of 'The Temple of Universal Peace Amongst Men' the reverse of evil, the same with many symbolic symbols like the swastika, this has opposite meanings, good and bad in different eras of history.

Thoth was the watcher and believed to be the maker of the emerald tablet. In the time of Alexandria the Great in his secret library 13 unique tablets where held, one being made of an indestructible green rock like substance of unknown origin or substance. The tablet was carved before the deluge with the true writings and wisdom of Thoth. Thoth, it is written, lived and studied Earth some 36,000 years ago working with the Anunnaki. He was the watcher and he who accounted for all life on earth in the reign of the gods. The original tablet was lost, although it was believed to be hidden, but the writings were kept and replicas are accessible for the public to read in museums all around the world. The translation tells the story of man's creation by the Anunnaki and tells the truth and wisdom of the universe. It is something that should be digested and understood if you are also a seeker of truth.

These teachings and knowledge have influenced many of our known academics and scholars in history who have taken the time to source his secret wisdom. Wisdom and knowledge is not for all to see, only for the people who search.

The reason why the ancient cultures started with great knowledge and architecture and slowly declined, which is clear to see, is they had the ancient knowledge taught to them by an ancient superior master, as the centuries followed, the teachings were lost.

Pythagoras studied in Egypt for many years in the great temples, these temples were places of work for the initiated few involved with alchemic practises, not religion. His geometry texts were thought to be translations of Hermetic teachings not original ideas of his own, restatements of ancient Egyptian philosophy.

The Emerald Tablet with the original writing was discovered around 3,000 BC in the time of Alexander's world library. After the Romans destroyed the town the tablet was never seen again but the teachings where copied and can be seen today. Several versions of the Emerald Tablet of Hermes were in secret circulation and saved by the Jewish fraternity all over Europe, Asia and Russia so the sacred texts were preserved.

The Roman Catholic Church and Emperor Constantine smothered and eradicated the Hermetic teachings that the Egyptians and Greeks painstakingly gathered which put the world back 2,000 years; they have much to answer for. Many of the things we are inventing today are reinventions of what was known before. The whole Egyptian culture started wise and powerful through these teachings, this is why the knowledge of superior architecture was formed in these times well before our history books suggest. For example, the knowledge of the Kybalion the teaching of vibration, amongst other things, altering the solid state of mass and levitation. The origin of the Philosophers Stone and teachings were handed down by word of mouth scholar to scholar, kept in the inner circle. Although books where rarely written if you search deeply the basic principles can be found and studied. A book called the 'Kybalion Hermetic Philosophy' was published in 1908 under the pseudonym 'The Three Initiates' which gives the essence and a taste of the secret foundation.

This, according to the alchemists, is the law of nature that applies to everything including humans as all of man's evolution happens through the process of burning out the imperfections until a pure man can be born, free of the physical lusts and worldly temptations that make him imperfect.

MONATOMIC GOLD

One of the most intriguing unknown phenomena discovered in ancient scribes is a substance called 'Mfkzt' or Mana, used throughout ancient Egypt and Sumerian cultures. It is believed to be used to develop and access the parts of the brain we still do not understand. This substance is a white powder, derived from gold in its purist form, known as monatomic gold which brings enlightenment and spiritual passage which has been sought for centuries in the alchemy practices. It is thought by scientists today, to be the key to hyper dimensional environments and parallel dimensions, reaching far beyond the reality of space and time we understand today.

Different cultures had their own name for the powder, the Egyptians called it 'Mfkzt', the Alexandrians referred to it as the 'Paradise Stone' and in Mesopotamia it was called 'Shimada'. All cultures expressed the same belief that the magical powder could induce levitation, and perform acts of spiritual teleportation. It was believed to be the gateway to longevity and the connection and path way to the afterlife.

Contemporary studies show that matter can be in two places at one time, in different dimensions. It has been discovered that some matter is able to 'communicate' without any physical connection. There is a growing belief that space time can be manipulated and teleportation may become a reality.

As in alchemy, the gold is distilled to its purist form using heat techniques. But when the process is finished it does not register as gold, but as a strange unique form of silica, it changes its colour and medium to a fine, white powder. This matter does not appear on the Periodic Table of Elements, mono-atomic gold consists of tiny strings of atoms, clusters or micro clusters the same as DNA strands. These properties of mono-atomic gold have opened up all kinds of possibilities that were previously considered theories.

In ancient texts and Hieroglyphs 'Mana' is portrayed as a cone shaped vessel. Held by the kings and ancient clergy, it is associated with illumination, knowledge and wisdom. It is known that from around 2,800 BC the Pharaohs of Egypt were ingesting Mana in the form of bread which only the High Priests, the Great Artificers, knew how to prepare. Pharaohs ingested it to enhance longevity, and to take them spiritually to the next life.

In 1904, Flinders Petrie discovered an Egyptian cave considered to be a temple of work on Mount Serabit near Mount Sinai. Sinai was, according to the Bible the place of magic where Moses was said to have witnessed the 'Burning Bush', spoke with the gods and undertook the building of the Ark of the Covenant. Their belief was humans have a physical body, and also a light body, both bodies need to be nurtured to live a full life, speaking of the pineal gland, the third eye.

In the Egyptian 'Book of the Dead' (Ref.Sec.7), thought to date back to around 3,100 BC, it has a description of the magical Mana, it says:

'I am purified of all imperfections. What is it? I ascend the golden hawk of Horus. What is it? I pass by the immortals without dying. What is it? I come before my father in Heaven. What is it?'

The substance has been tested for conductivity and it was discovered to be a superconductor. A superconductor is a material that has a single wavelength, a single vibration or energy. A superconductor does not allow any voltage potential to exist within it, it is perfect current. In a superconductor the electrons pair up consisting of a time forward and a time reverse, when this happens they become light. Light may exist in any quantity in a superconductor, it does not reside in any space time, this is Einstein's theory of past, present and future, relativity.

The Ark of the Covenant, the throne of the returning god, the most powerful object ever used on earth was known to use Mana or monatomic gold as its power source generating vast amounts of current. It is believed that this technology was used to levitate stone combining the natural energies of the earth and ionosphere, the lost knowledge of nature's power.

This is not the only time in history where hallucinogenic or mind-altering drugs have been used for peering into closed dimensions. The psilocybin cactus of South America is still used by the shamans to access the spirit world to consult with their ancestors for guidance and knowledge. Many drugs have been used to gain passage to the spirit world to be enlightened of our true being. Joining together as people and experiencing the Mandelbrot theory in a real life condition is truly a marvel and worldly experience. These mind enhancing substances which are found naturally in nature have been banned from society, suppressing spiritual enlightenment. Only medication prescribed by doctors which produce large amounts of revenue are allowed in today's society.

CONCLUSION

The world is being divided up into ten unions for the purpose of world control. The agenda is to unite southern America with the North American states; the Middle Eastern countries will eventually be under one ruling body. Europe is already controlled and being led by the new world rule. South Asia, East Asia, Africa, the Pacific and Russia will be unions under one world governing body if the NWO succeeds. The preparations as predicted and planned by many for world domination are well underway with World War 3 looming. Create world chaos and destruction of the old system and offer an alternative that the people can't refuse, this is the agenda of the New World Order.

Iceland, a country that has shown initiative in bringing the bankers of their country to justice without corruption in their judicial system prevailing, is a lesson to us all that it can be achieved. United we stand, divided we fall.

Who are the people who truly rule our world, the people who control the world's banks and finances, the people who manufacture war for personal gain and send innocent solders to kill innocent people to gain land and power? Who are the people who wish to control our food supply, regiment and suppress the world's population and gain full control of all finances and land?

The beneficiaries of the wealthiest corporations in the worlds and the banks that hold and loan their money are the true masters of our system, these are the people who truly rule as a shadow world government.

In 1954 a group of wealthy business men, politicians, media companies and international royalty set up a secret company called 'The Bilderberg Group' meeting for the first time in Oosterbeek, Netherlands with the founding father being Prince Burnhard of the Netherlands. The agenda for the Bilderbergs is to realise the dream of their forefathers to control and own all finances as one private group of people. The grand design is for a One World Government with a single global marketplace, policed by one world army, being financially regulated by a central bank using one global electronic currency.

The Bilderberg Group has a membership representing the world's leading financial corporate power elites, an estimated group of 2,000 people. Mostly American, Canadian, and western European familiar names like David Rockefeller, Henry Kissinger, Bill Clinton, Gordon Brown, Angela Merkel, Alan Greenspan, Ben Bernanke, Larry Summers, Tim Geithner, Lloyd Blankfein, George Soros, Donald Rumsfeld, Rupert Murdoch, influential senators, congressmen, parliamentarians, NATO chiefs and members of European royalty. This group all attend or have attended meetings. No agenda or discussed topics become public or any public media or press coverage is allowed, all attendees are sworn to secrecy and guests are explicitly forbidden from giving interviews to journalists or divulge any criteria discussed in the meetings. These people own the media companies that report the biased news given to us daily, no news is sacred.

Welcome to 'Agenda 21', this is the start of the new legislation of world control and the breaking down of all human rights and personal freedom. It has been decided that the world's people are unable to look after themselves, so we are to be owned. It is the new legislation that has been put forward and is now in motion concerning the unity of all countries being governed by one world cult, 'The New World Order'. The NWO is not new and it will not create order, greed is a thirst that is never quenched. The path that our race has chosen will destroy itself unless the parasitic cancer of greed and power is removed from the rule of our kind.

Much of this book is explaining the past deeds of the ruling class of this world; if you are unconvinced please study Agenda 21 which quite clearly states your future of non-human rights and freedom, sold to us through the deception of public security and climate control.

We should unplug from the system that we are fed and view the bigger picture, educate ourselves and learn the truth instead of being led on a pointless, monotonous one-way path of life with selected media garbage, enlighten ourselves and set ourselves free.

At the Bilderberg Group meeting of 1992 Henry Kissinger was purported to have said:-

"Today, Americans would be outraged if UN troops entered Los Angeles to restore order, tomorrow they will be grateful. This is especially true if they were told there was an outside threat from beyond, whether real or promulgated, that threatened our very existence. It is then that all people of the world will plead with world leaders to deliver them from this evil. Individual rights will be willingly relinquished for the guarantee of their well-being granted to them by their world government".

For myself the world has gone and got itself much too serious, with too many dark forces at play crushing the beauty and freedom of living life. We need to unite and discuss as a race these ugly realities which are quickly looming. For these globalists to succeed they rely on participation of the people. The true terrorists are the ones making the rules, take the power back, connect via the web and speak as one body. Stop the war and corruption. If we choose freedom and stop, they have nothing to rule.

BIBLIOGRAPHY AND REFERENCES

Author: Zachariah Sitchin

Book Tittle: Divine Encounters

Published By: Avon Books

Published: 31st July 1998 (Reissue edition)

Author: Zachariah Sitchin

Book tittle: There Were Giants Upon This Earth

Published by: Bear and Company

Published: 5th May 2010

****

Author: Helena Blavatsky

Book tittle: The Secret Doctrine (First edition 1888)

Published by: Tarcher Perigee

Published: July 23rd 2009

****

Author: Adolf Hitler

Book tittle: Mien Kampf: My Struggle (translation)

Published by: Liberty Bell

Published: 22nd February 2004

****

(Ref. Sec.1)

Author: Robert Sepehr

Book tittle: 1666 Redemption Through Sin

Published by: Atlantian Gardens (first edition)

Published: 15th May 2015

****

Author: Manly P. Hall

Book tittle: The Secret Destiny of America

Published by: Penguin Putnam Inc. Jeremy P. Tarcher

Published: 1st October 2008

****

Author: Arthur C. Clarke

Book tittle: Profiles of the Future

Published by: Phoenix

Published: 14th December 2000

****

Author: Enoch

Book title: The Book of Enoch (Translation)

Publisher: Fifth estate incorporated

Published: 10th October 2011

****

Author: George Orwell

Book title: 1984 Nineteen Eighty Four

Publisher: Penguin Classics: New Edition.

Published: 29th January 2004

****

Author: Altus Eli Luminosus Aequallis P.J.L.

Book tittle: Mutus Liber Loquitur

Published by: Saucer Eqestris Aurems Ordo Inc.

Published: October 16th 2013

****

Author: Stephen Flowers (Edited by)

Book tittle: Hermetic Magic

Published by: Red Wheel / Weiser

Published: 14th December 1995

****

(Ref.Sec.2)

Search reference: Fractural Mandelbrot

The Explanation and Position of Our Physical Existence in the Universe.

(You Tube Search)

****

(Ref. Sec. 3)

Author: Annie Jacobsen

Book tittle: Operation Paperclip

Published By: New York: Little Brown and Company

Published: 2014

****

(Ref.sec.4)

Anomaly on the Surface of the Sun (March 8th 2012)

https:www.youtube.com/watch?v=PYHZV-QpRLs

(Or: You tube search "Anomaly refuelling on the surface of the sun, NASA March 8th 2012")

****

Ref. Sec.5)

Author: Albert Pike

Book tittle: Morals and Dogma of the Ancient and Accepted Scottish Rite of Freemasonry

Published by: Martino Fine Books

Published: July 11th 2013

****

(Ref. Sec. 6)

Author: Jacque Fresco (futurist and social engineer)

Book tittle: The Venus Project (The Redesign of a Culture)

Published by: Global Cyber- Visions

Published: 1 June 1995

****

(Ref. Sec. 7)

Author: John Romer

Book tittle: Egyptian Book of the Dead

Published by: Penguin Books Ltd

Published: 28th August 2008

****

(Ref. Sec. 8)

Author: Max Planck (Noble prize winner in Physics)

Book tittle: Where is Science Going?

Published by: Muriwai Books

Published: June 28th 2017 (First published 1932)

DISCLAIMER

All rights to this publication are reserved. No part may be reproduced, copied or translated in any form without prior permission of the copyright owner and author.

Neither the author, publisher or editor shall have any liability to any person or entity with respect to any loss or damage caused by or alleged to be caused directly or indirectly by acting or referring from actions due to the contents of this book.

Although all information written in this publication 'The World Is Not Ending But' has been selected from factual sources, it should be used responsibly and at a person's discretion. Personal reference, study and clarification are advised for your own peace of mind.

Copyright © By Jack Grey. All rights reserved

Published 23 February 2018

Printed in Great Britain
by Amazon